# THE FAN OVEN BOOK

# THE FAN OVEN
# BOOK

## WITH RECIPES

Jenny Webb

**RIGHT WAY**

Typeset in 10/11 pt Swiss 721 by Letterpart Ltd., Reigate, Surrey.

Printed and bound in Great Britain by Cox & Wyman Ltd., Reading, Berkshire.

The *Right Way* series is published by Elliot Right Way Books, Brighton Road, Lower Kingswood, Tadworth, Surrey, KT20 6TD, U.K. For information about our company and the other books we publish, visit our web site at www.right-way.co.uk

# CONTENTS

# DEDICATION

My thanks go to NEFF and Stoves plc for providing me with information concerning the recent design and use of forced air convection ovens.

To Jo Smith and Joanna and Peter Stephen-Ward for their support, encouragement and willingness to eat and comment on the numerous recipes.

To Judith Mitchell for her editing talent.

To Annie Willis for her splendid illustrations.

# INTRODUCTION

An electric oven is an electric oven, or is it? In recent years there has been a tremendous development within the cooker industry, and often this has led to the cook experiencing heartache and frustration, especially when attempting to cook old, tried and tested, favourite recipes in a new oven.

For most of us, if there is an explanation and some guidance on any subject, life becomes easier. Thus, the purpose of this book is to look at fan ovens, to appreciate how they work and compare the differences between them and conventional ovens.

The recipes cover most of the basic British fare but also include many others which have now become a part of the UK's international cuisine.

I hope that my explanations will help you to understand how your oven works and what you can do to get the best from it.

Jenny Webb

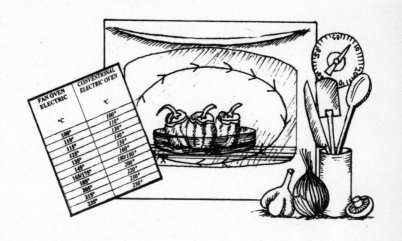

# Part One

# UNDERSTANDING THE PRINCIPLES

# 1

# THE DIFFERENCES BETWEEN A FAN AND A CONVENTIONAL OVEN

Cooking in an oven is a natural process. As the air in the oven is heated, it produces convection currents. The hotter air rises to the top whilst the cooler air can be found at the bottom of the oven. As the heat penetrates the food, the outside browns and the inside cooks and so becomes edible and suitable for the human digestive system. Depending on the type of food and temperature used, the process may be short or long.

Conventional ovens use this natural process and, to get the best results, instructions are given which indicate the specific shelf position to use. Older recipe instructions may simply give guidance; for example, they may merely suggest using the top, middle or bottom of the oven.

Fan ovens, technically known as 'forced air convection ovens', use the same natural principle but by placing a fan inside the oven the air is moved more quickly and evenly around it. The fan is usually situated in the vicinity of the heating source and will circulate the heat from either the sides or the back of the oven.

Although the noise of the fan may sound as if the air is being blasted around the oven, the movement of air is actually very gentle.

The cook gets many benefits from using a fan oven, as you'll see in the next chapter. It's important that you are aware of these, especially if you have only previously used a conventional oven. Manufacturers often supply a recipe book, which should be followed, but problems sometimes arise when you want to use a recipe which was originated for a conventional oven.

The following pages give simple explanations on the various aspects of using a fan oven, which will help you to use both old and new recipes.

# 2

# USING CONVENTIONAL
# RECIPES IN A FAN OVEN

**Shelf Positions – Don't Worry**
As the air in a fan oven is evenly distributed, there is no need to worry about which shelf position to use. An additional bonus is that all the shelves can be used at the same time. This is very useful when cooking bulk quantities, perhaps for the freezer or for an event where a large quantity of food is needed.

**Cooking from Cold – It can be Done**
With the aid of a fan, the oven heats up more quickly than a conventional oven so preheating is of lesser importance. Even so, some recipes, particularly cakes and pastries, are cooked better by preheating first. Should you decide to cook from cold you may need to add about 5-10 minutes to the overall cooking time. Unless the cooker manufacturer gives specific instructions to cook from frozen, food must be thawed before cooking.

**Oven Temperatures – Are Different**
When cooking in a fan oven, the internal oven temperatures may be 10-20 degrees lower than those used in a conventional oven. To use a favourite conventional recipe, check in the manufacturer's recipe book or check the chart given on page 16 for guidance.

**Cooking Times – Are Faster**
As the oven heats up so quickly, the cooking operation becomes faster so, when using your own recipes, reduce the cooking time by about 10 minutes for every hour of cooking.

## Saving Energy – No Effort Required

You do nothing, simply enjoy the fact that the oven is cooking more quickly and, if you wish, you can cook more at the same time. The amount of energy used will be less, which means money is also saved.

# 3

# OVEN TEMPERATURE CONVERSION CHART

**How to Use the Chart**
Overleaf is the oven temperature conversion chart. Select the conventional temperature from the appropriate column (given in *italics*), then match it with the suggested fan oven temperature (given in **bold**). For circotherm temperature settings, refer to page 17, Recipe Notes.

**The Oven Thermostat**
While the oven is heating, an indicator light will be 'on'. When the oven has reached the temperature selected on the oven control dial, the light will go 'out'.

During the cooking period, the light will come 'on' and go 'out' at intervals. This shows that the oven temperature is being maintained.

| Gas Mark | Fan Oven Electric °C | Conventional Electric Oven °C | Conventional Electric Oven °F |
|---|---|---|---|
| 1/4 | 100° | 100° | 200° |
| 1/4 | 110° | 110° | 225° |
| 1/2 | 115° | 130° | 250° |
| 1 | 125° | 140° | 275° |
| 2 | 135° | 150° | 300° |
| 3 | 145° | 160° | 325° |
| 4-5 | 165/175° | 180/190° | 350/375° |
| 6 | 185° | 200° | 400° |
| 7 | 205° | 220° | 425° |
| 8 | 215° | 230° | 450° |
| 9 | 235° | 250° | 475° |

*Important*
The conversion chart is for guidance only. Slight variations can be expected.

# 4

# RECIPE NOTES

**Temperature Settings**
All the recipes in this book have been tested in a standard electric fan oven. If you are using a Circotherm electric oven or a Circotherm gas oven, you'll need to convert the temperatures using your manufacturer's chart.

**Measurements of Ingredients**
Although metric measurements are officially in use, you may prefer to use imperial measures. For your convenience both are quoted. However, as the conversions have been altered to make weighing easier, it is important to remember only to use either and not to skip from one to the other in any one recipe, otherwise the recipe will not be successful.

**Ingredients**
All the recipes have been tested to give the best possible guidance to the cook but it has to be accepted that the individual ingredient will vary. For example: flour, depending on its storage conditions, may absorb slightly more or less liquid; eggs of the same size will not have a precise weight; fats will mix differently depending on whether they have been stored in a refrigerator or not; and even the kitchen temperature can have a bearing on the ingredients. To help to rule out as many variables as possible it is worth using the same brand of ingredients and, unless stated to the contrary, condition them in the kitchen for at least two hours before compiling the recipe.

**Preparation of Cake Tins**
Where the recipe calls for a tin to be greased and lined, lightly grease the inside of the tin with butter or margarine

and then line with greaseproof paper. To do this, cut out a circle to fit the base of the tin and then a long strip to cover the total circumference of the tin. This strip lining should be about 5cm/2 inches higher than the depth of the tin. Place the strip on a flat surface and make a horizontal fold of about 2.5cm/1 inch. Using scissors, cut diagonally at about 2.5cm/1 inch intervals up to the point where the paper is folded. Arrange the lining around the inside of the tin and then place the circle of paper on the base.

*To grease and flour a tin*
Grease the inside with butter or margarine and sprinkle about a teaspoon of flour over the base. Then, tap the sides of the tin, both while holding the tin level and while moving it slightly up and down, to coat all the inside surfaces evenly. Tip the tin upside down and tap on a hard surface to get rid of any excess flour.

## Using the Oven
Each oven has its own characteristics and, once you are familiar with them, you will be aware of any slight adjustments you may need to make to suit your recipes. If you don't select the exact correct temperature on the control dial each time you use it, the thermostat will, of course, operate slightly differently. If the kitchen is very hot or cold, this will affect the heating up time.

*When preheating:* The oven is preheated when the indicator light goes 'out'.

The heat distribution of the oven has been engineered to give the best possible circulation. Never line shelves or cover the oven interior with foil as the oven will not perform correctly.

Before heating the oven, remove any oven furniture that is not required – that includes oven shelves and baking trays or dishes. Why waste time and electricity heating things which are not needed?

## The Fan Oven
The fan oven has been sold since the late 1960s and there are still many old models in use today. The latest ovens are so fast that preheating takes only a few minutes and, as a result, most do not require to be preheated. However, I have tried to take into account both the old and new models and thus given some indication in each recipe as to any adjustments you

may need to make to suit your oven. If you have a manufacturer's handbook, it is worth checking the instructions in it as most manufacturers test their own models and give specific instructions to help you get the best from them.

## Roasting Tips

Always ensure that the meat, poultry or game is completely thawed before cooking. This ensures a better-cooked result and reduces splashing in the oven.

To reduce splashing and smoking during cooking, use a large meat tin for very large joints and birds, and a smaller one for the smaller quantities.

Roasting bags and foil can be used but follow the manufacturer's instructions if you want to achieve the best result.

Many years ago water used to be added to the roasting tin. With modern ovens this is unnecessary.

Some meat is naturally tough. To tenderize it, marinate it for several hours before cooking. You can either rub the meat with the marinade or immerse it. A basic marinade is two tablespoons of oil to one tablespoon of vinegar or lemon juice.

Joints and poultry can be carved more easily if left to stand for 10-15 minutes after cooking.

When roasting large joints of meat or poultry, the oven can be turned off about 10 minutes before the end of the cooking time to save even more energy.

Stuffing poultry is not advised as there could be a chance that the meat around the stuffing is not sufficiently cooked. Should you want to use a stuffing, then stuff the neck end where there is sufficient loose skin to contain it.

## Baking Tips

Cakes are best made in a warm kitchen; the room temperature should not be below 17-20°C/65-70°F.

All the ingredients should be at room temperature except for a fat being used for a rubbing in mixture which should be used straight from the refrigerator.

Most recipes for cakes and pastries are best cooked after the oven is preheated.

Use the tin and container sizes given in a recipe. If you have to use a different size, be prepared for a slightly different cooking time and possibly a different result.

Self raising flours and raising agents such as baking powder, bicarbonate of soda and cream of tartar should be as fresh as possible as they lose their strength with overlong storage.

# Part 2

# RECIPES

# 5

# FISH

# Baked Savoury Sole

If using a preheated oven, you may need to reduce the cooking time by about 5-10 minutes.

*Serves 4*

*Preparation and Cooking Time: 45-50 minutes*

**4 sole fillets with a total weight of 500g/1 lb 2 oz**
**1 tbsp lemon juice**
**4 tomatoes, sliced**
**Salt and pepper**
**2 tbsp fresh white breadcrumbs**
**25g/1 oz Cheddar cheese, finely grated**

1.  Place the fish in a buttered, shallow, ovenproof dish.

2.  Sprinkle the lemon juice over the fish and arrange slices of tomato on each.

3.  Season to taste. Sprinkle over the breadcrumbs and then the cheese.

4.  Cook from cold at 150°C for 25-30 minutes or until the cheese is golden.

# Spicy Haddock

If using a preheated oven you may need to reduce the cooking time by about 5-10 minutes.

For a change, cod fillets could be used as a substitute for the haddock.

*Serves 4*

*Preparation and Cooking Time: 1¼-1½ hours*

**2 tbsp vegetable oil**
**1 small onion, peeled and chopped**
**1 clove garlic, crushed**
**2 tbsp soy sauce**
**1 level tsp mixed dried herbs**
**½ tsp curry powder**
**260g/9 oz can chopped tomatoes, with juice**
**50g/2 oz button mushrooms, sliced**
**Salt and pepper**
**550g/1¼ lb haddock fillet, skinned and cut into pieces**

1.  Heat the oil in a pan and gently cook the onion and garlic until the onion is soft.

2.  Stir in the soy sauce, herbs, curry powder, tomatoes and juice and mushrooms. Season to taste.

3.  Place the fish into a buttered 1 litre/2 pt casserole dish, pour over the sauce, cover and cook from cold at 150°C for 60-70 minutes or until the fish is cooked.

# Tuna and Corn Pizza

If using a preheated oven, you may need to reduce the cooking time by about 5-10 minutes.

*Makes 1 × 30cm/12 inch pizza*

*Preparation and Cooking Time: 50-60 minutes*

**2 tbsp olive or vegetable oil**
**1 large onion, peeled and chopped**
**1 clove garlic, crushed**
**4 large tomatoes, sliced**
**1 level tbsp dried basil**
**1 small (100g/4 oz) can of tuna, drained and flaked**
**1 tbsp canned corn**
**Salt and pepper**
**2 tbsp tomato purée**
**1 × 30cm/12 inch ready-made pizza base**
**50g/2 oz Cheddar cheese, grated**
**6 black olives, stoned and cut into quarters**

1.  Heat the oil in a pan and gently cook the onion and garlic until soft.

2.  Add the tomatoes and basil. Cook for about 5 minutes. Remove from the heat.

3.  Gently stir in the tuna and corn, and season to taste. Spread the tomato purée over the base.

4.  Cover the pizza base with the tuna mixture, then with the grated cheese.

5.  Sprinkle over the olives and cook from cold at a temperature of 160°C for 20-25 minutes.

# Crab and Prawn Puffs

If using a preheated oven, you may need to reduce the cooking time by about 5-10 minutes.

These are also good to serve cold for picnics and lunch boxes.

*Serves 4*

*Preparation and Cooking Time: 45-60 minutes*

**25g/1 oz butter or margarine, melted**
**1 tsp plain flour**
**90ml/3 fl oz single cream**
**100g/4 oz crabmeat**
**125g/5 oz prawns, shelled**
**½ tsp lemon juice**
**½ tsp curry powder**
**Salt and pepper**

**225g/8 oz frozen puff or flaky pastry, thawed**
**1 medium egg, lightly beaten**

1.  Melt the butter in a pan and stir in the flour until it has absorbed the butter. Stir in the cream and gently cook for 2-3 minutes.

2.  Stir in the crabmeat, prawns, lemon juice and curry powder, and season to taste.

3.  Roll the pastry into a large 30cm/12 inch square, then cut into four. On each piece of pastry spread some crab mixture but leave the edges.

4.  Brush the edges with egg and diagonally fold each piece of pastry over the filling. Crimp the edges to seal and brush with egg.

5.  Place onto a baking sheet and bake from cold at 190°C for 15-20 minutes or until golden brown.

# Oven-Baked Sardine Toasted Sandwiches

If using a preheated oven, you may need to reduce the cooking time by about 5-10 minutes.

*Serves 4-6*

*Preparation and Cooking Time: 45-50 minutes*

**12 slices medium-cut sliced bread, crusts removed**
**Butter or margarine for spreading**
**100g/4 oz cream cheese**
**Grated rind of 1 lemon**
**120g/4¼ oz can sardines, drained**
**6 green olives, stoned and finely chopped**
**Salt and pepper**
**100g/4 oz Cheddar cheese, grated**

1.  Butter both sides of the bread.

2.  Combine in a bowl the cream cheese, lemon rind, sardines and olives, and season to taste.

3.  Spread the sardine mixture over the slices of bread and cut each slice into four triangles.

4.  Place the triangles onto the wire oven shelf with the roasting pan underneath. Sprinkle over the cheese.

5.  Cook from cold at 190°C for 20-25 minutes or until the tops and undersides are golden brown.

# Foil-Baked Salmon

If using a preheated oven, you may need to reduce the cooking time by about 5-10 minutes.

*Serves 8-12 depending on the size of the salmon*

*Preparation Time: 15 minutes*

*Cooking Time: allow 24 minutes per kg or 12 minutes per lb*

**1 whole salmon, cleaned and gutted**
**Butter or margarine**
**Salt and pepper**
**1 lemon, cut into slices**
**Bunch of parsley**
**Juice of 1 lemon**

1. Tear off a piece of foil twice the size of the salmon and grease thoroughly with butter.

2. Season the salmon inside and out, and place on the foil.

3. Place the lemon slices and the parsley inside the body cavity. Pour the juice over the salmon.

4. Enclose the salmon in the foil, tightly sealing the edges.

5. Place in a roasting pan and cook from cold at 160°C allowing 24 minutes per kg or 12 minutes per lb.

# Fish Cannelloni

If using a preheated oven, you may need to reduce the cooking time by about 5-10 minutes.

Many associate the traditional cannelloni with a meat filling but for lovers of fish or non-meat-eaters this is an interesting change. Canned tuna, pink salmon or flaked cooked white fish can be used as a substitute for the salmon.

*Serves 4*

*Preparation and Cooking Time: 1-1¼ hours*

**425g/1 lb canned salmon, drained and mashed**
**120ml/4 fl oz crème fraîche**
**Salt and pepper**

*Sauce*
**25g/1 oz butter or margarine**
**25g/1 oz plain flour**
**550ml/1 pt milk**
**100g/4 oz Mozzarella cheese, grated**

**12 cannelloni tubes**
**Grated nutmeg**

1.  Mix together the salmon and crème fraîche in a bowl. Season to taste.

2.  Melt the butter in a pan and stir in the flour, gradually add the milk and cook until smooth and thick. Stir in 75g/3 oz cheese until melted. Season to taste.

3.  Place the salmon mixture in a piping bag with a plain nozzle. Pipe the mixture into the tubes. If preferred, use a teaspoon to fill the tubes.

4.  Arrange the tubes in a shallow, buttered dish and pour over the sauce. Sprinkle with the remaining cheese and grate over the nutmeg. Cook from cold at 170°C for 35-40 minutes or until the cheese is golden brown and bubbling.

# Salmon in Cream

If using a preheated oven, you may need to reduce the cooking time by about 5-10 minutes.

Cod or haddock steaks can be used as a substitute for the salmon.

*Serves 4*

*Preparation and Cooking Time: 30-45 minutes*

**4 salmon steaks with a total weight of 500g/1 lb 2 oz**
**40g/1½ oz butter or margarine**
**Salt and pepper**
**284ml/10 fl oz single cream**
**Grated rind of 1 lemon**
**1 heaped tbsp fresh dill leaves**

1.  Place the steaks in a buttered, shallow, ovenproof dish, dot with butter and season to taste.

2.  Pour over the cream to cover the steaks, sprinkle over the rind and dill leaves. Cover with a lid or foil.

3.  Cook from cold at 150°C for 20-25 minutes or until cooked. If required, baste with the cream during cooking.

# Pilchard and Tomato Loaf

If using a preheated oven, you may need to reduce the cooking time by about 5-10 minutes.

This makes an inexpensive nutritious meal, which can be served hot or cold. It is also a useful recipe for picnics or lunch boxes.

*Serves 4*

*Preparation and Cooking Time: 1¼-1½ hours*

**15g/½ oz butter or margarine, melted**
**425g/16 oz can pilchards, drained**
**400g/15 oz can chopped tomatoes**
**1 small onion, peeled and finely chopped**
**50g/2 oz fresh brown breadcrumbs**
**2 level tsp dried mixed herbs**
**2 medium eggs, lightly beaten**
**Salt and pepper**

1.  Line a 650g/1½ lb loaf tin with foil and brush with the butter.

2.  In a bowl, mix together the pilchards, tomatoes, onion, breadcrumbs, herbs and eggs. Season to taste. Transfer to the loaf tin and smooth over the top.

3.  Cook from cold at 180°C for 45-50 minutes. Allow to cool before turning out onto a serving dish.

# Fish and Potato Pie

If using a preheated oven, you may need to reduce the cooking time by about 5-10 minutes.

Any white fish can be used or, to 'posh' it up, add two chopped scallops and 50g/2 oz shelled prawns and, instead of milk, use a dry white wine.

*Serves 4*

*Preparation and Cooking Time: 1¼-1½ hours*

Sauce
**25g/1 oz butter or margarine**
**25g/1 oz flour**
**285ml/½ pt milk**
**2 tsp parsley, chopped**
**Salt and pepper**

**350g/12 oz cooked white fish, boned and cut into**
   **1cm/½ inch cubes**
**2 tbsp milk**
**15g/½ oz butter or margarine**
**450g/1 lb potatoes, cooked and mashed**

1.  Melt 25g/1 oz butter in a saucepan and stir in the flour, gradually add the milk and cook until smooth and thick. Add the parsley and season to taste.

2.  Mix in the fish and pour into a buttered 690ml/1¼ pt dish.

3.  Warm the milk and 15g/½ oz butter together in a pan and beat into the potatoes.

4.  Pile over the fish mixture and smooth with a fork.

5.  Cook from cold at 170°C for 35-40 minutes or until golden brown.

# Russian Fish Pie

If using a preheated oven, you may need to reduce the cooking time by about 5-10 minutes.

This recipe can be served either hot or cold.

*Serves 4*

*Preparation and Cooking Time: 50-55 minutes*

**340g/¾ lb frozen puff pastry, thawed**
**450g/1 lb cooked white fish, boned and flaked**
**2 tbsp crème fraîche**
**1 tbsp parsley, chopped**
**Salt and pepper**
**1 tomato, sliced into quarters**
**1 hard boiled egg with shell removed and cut into**
**   quarters**

*Glaze*
**1 medium egg, lightly beaten**

1.  On a floured board, roll the pastry to a 30cm/12 inch square, trimming the edges. Cut and divide into four squares.

2.  In a bowl, mix the fish with the crème fraîche and parsley. Season to taste. Divide the mixture into four and place this mixture onto the centre of each square of pastry. Place quarters of tomato and egg on top of the fish mixture.

3.  Brush edges with beaten egg. Fold the pastry into an envelope shape over the mixture and seal.

4.  Roll the pastry trimmings out thinly and cut into leaves. Brush with egg and arrange on the top of each pie.

5.  Make small slits on the top of each pie to allow the steam to escape. Place on a greased baking sheet and cook from cold at 190°C for 20 minutes, then reduce the temperature to 150°C and cook for a further 10-15 minutes.

# Baked Cod

If using a preheated oven, you may need to reduce the cooking time by about 5-10 minutes.

Salmon steaks could be used as a substitute for the cod.

*Serves 4*

*Preparation and Cooking Time: 45-60 minutes*

**50g/2 oz fresh white breadcrumbs**
**1 tbsp parsley, chopped**
**Salt and pepper**
**4 cod steaks with a total weight of 500g/1 lb 2 oz**
**1 medium egg, lightly beaten**
**25g/1 oz butter**

1.  In a bowl, mix the breadcrumbs, parsley, salt and pepper to taste.

2.  Brush the steaks with egg, and coat with the breadcrumbs.

3.  Place a knob of butter on each steak and place in a greased shallow ovenproof dish.

4.  Cook from cold at 150°C for 35-40 minutes.

# Baked Trout with Toasted Almonds

If using a preheated oven, you may need to reduce the cooking time by about 5-10 minutes.

*Serves 4*

*Preparation and Cooking Time: 40-55 minutes*

**4 trout about 350g/12 oz each, cleaned and gutted**
**Juice of 1 lemon**
**25g/1 oz butter or margarine**
**50g/2 oz ready toasted almonds**

1.  Place the fish in a buttered, shallow, ovenproof dish. Pour over the lemon juice and dot each trout with butter.

2.  Cover and cook from cold at 150°C for 35-40 minutes or until the fish is cooked.

3.  Serve sprinkled with toasted almonds.

# Poached Smoked Haddock

If using a preheated oven, you may need to reduce the cooking time by about 5-10 minutes.

To serve as a traditional breakfast dish, place a poached egg on the top of each fish just before serving. Most white fish can be poached in this manner.

*Serves 4*

*Preparation and Cooking Time: 40-45 minutes*

**450-550g/1-1¼ lb smoked haddock fillets**
**Salt and pepper**
**285ml/½ pt milk**
**50g/2 oz butter or margarine**

1. Wash the fish and place in a shallow ovenproof dish. Season to taste.

2. Pour over the milk and place a piece of butter on each fillet. Cover with foil. Cook from cold at 150°C for 25-30 minutes.

# Mackerel in Cider

If using a preheated oven, you may need to reduce the cooking time by about 5-10 minutes.

Oily fish, such as mackerel, need the addition of an acid to temper the oil, which is why cider or apple juice is used here. If using apple juice, avoid any which contains added sugar as this will be too sweet. If buying whole mackerel, ask the fishmonger to bone and fillet them.

*Serves 4*

*Preparation and Cooking Time: 65-70 minutes*

**2 mackerel fillets with a total weight of 375g/13 oz**
**1 bay leaf**
**6 peppercorns**
**330ml/11 fl oz cider or apple juice**
**2 dessert apples, peeled, cored, and cut into rings**

1.  Place the fish into a 1 litre/2 pt casserole dish, add the bay leaf and peppercorns, and pour over the cider.

2.  Place the apple rings on top of the fish.

3.  Cover the casserole and cook from cold at 170°C for 35-40 minutes or until the fish starts to separate. Remove with a slotted spoon. Serve with a little of the sauce spooned over the fillets.

# Plaice in Wine with Grapes

If using a preheated oven, you may need to reduce the cooking time by about 5-10 minutes.

If preferred, the skin may be left on but the taste will not be so delicate.

To remove the skin: Place the fillet skin side down on a board, hold the tip of the tail and, with a sharp knife, ease the fish away from the skin.

*Serves 4*

*Preparation and Cooking Time: 65-70 minutes*

**4 large plaice fillets with a total weight of 375g/13 oz, skinned**
**Salt and pepper**
**1 onion, peeled and very finely chopped**
**100g/4 oz button mushrooms, wiped and sliced**
**200ml/7 fl oz crème fraîche**
**150ml/¼ pt dry white wine**
**50g/2 oz white seedless grapes, halved**

1. Roll up the plaice fillets tail first. Place in an ovenproof dish. Season to taste with salt and pepper.

2. Sprinkle over the onion and mushrooms.

3. Mix the crème fraîche and wine together in a jug, and pour over the fish.

4. Sprinkle over the grapes.

5. Cover the dish with foil and cook from cold at 170°C for 35-40 minutes or until the fish is opaque.

# Smoked Salmon Quiche

This recipe can be served warm or cold. For a variation, use cooked and flaked smoked haddock and/or choose a cream cheese with other flavourings. I find it easier to chop the smoked salmon with kitchen scissors.

*Serves 6-8*

*Preparation and Cooking Time: 1-1¼ hours*

**225g/8 oz frozen shortcrust pastry, thawed**
**100g/4 oz cream cheese with garlic and herbs**
**3 medium eggs**
**Scant 225ml/8 fl oz milk**
**Pepper**
**175g/6 oz smoked salmon, chopped**

1.  On a floured board roll out the pastry, if necessary, and line a 21cm/8½ inch flan case. Prick the base and bake blind in a preheated oven at 180°C for 15-20 minutes or until cooked but not overbrowned.

2.  Meanwhile, place the cheese in a bowl and beat until softened. Beat in the eggs one at a time. Stir in the milk and season to taste with pepper.

3.  Evenly sprinkle the salmon over the base of the pastry case and pour the milk mixture over.

4.  Bake for 30-35 minutes or until the top is browned and firm to the touch. Stand for 5 minutes before serving.

# 6

# MEAT, POULTRY AND GAME

# Turkey Loaf

This recipe can be cooked from cold but you may need to add about 5-10 minutes to the cooking time.

It is a good recipe for using up left over turkey or chicken, especially around the festive season. It can be eaten hot or cold and served with vegetables, salad or crispy bread.

*Serves 4-6*

*Preparation and Cooking Time: 1-1½ hours*

**7 streaky bacon rashers, rinds removed**
**25g/1 oz butter or margarine**
**1 medium onion, peeled and finely chopped**
**75g/3 oz fresh white breadcrumbs**
**1 level tsp dried tarragon**
**350g/12 oz cooked turkey, finely chopped**
**140ml/¼ pt chicken stock**
**2 medium eggs, lightly beaten**
**Salt and pepper**

1.  Stretch the rashers of bacon with the back of a knife and line the base and sides of a 15cm/6 inch soufflé dish with the bacon.

2.  Melt the butter in a pan and lightly fry the onion.

3.  Place the breadcrumbs in a bowl and stir in the onion and butter, tarragon, turkey, stock and eggs. Season to taste.

4.  Pour the mixture into the bacon-lined dish and bake in a preheated oven at 160°C for 45-60 minutes.

# Lamb's Liver Casserole

This recipe can be cooked from cold but you may need to add about 5-10 minutes to the cooking time.

Other liver such as pig's can be used but it has a very strong flavour and is less popular than lamb's liver.

*Serves 4*

*Preparation and Cooking Time: 1-1¼ hours*

**25g/1 oz butter or margarine**
**2 tsp vegetable oil**
**450g/1 lb lamb's liver, sliced**
**25g/1 oz flour, seasoned with salt and pepper**
**4 streaky bacon rashers, rinds removed, and chopped**
**1 large carrot, peeled and sliced**
**1 medium onion, peeled and chopped**
**2 tomatoes, quartered**
**285ml/½ pt lamb stock**
**2 tbsp tomato sauce**
**2 level tsp dried oregano**
**Salt and pepper**

1.  Heat the butter and oil in a pan. Toss the liver in the seasoned flour and fry to seal. Place in a casserole dish.

2.  Stir the bacon, carrot and onion together in the pan. Gently fry the vegetables until the onion is soft.

3.  Add the tomatoes and stir in the stock, tomato sauce and oregano. Bring to the boil, season to taste and pour over the liver.

4.  Cover and cook in a preheated oven at 170°C for 45-55 minutes or until the vegetables are tender.

# Rabbit Pie

I buy diced frozen rabbit at the supermarket but, should you wish to use a fresh rabbit, cut it into joints, stew until tender with vegetables and then dice. Use the stock for the sauce.

*Serves 4*

*Preparation and Cooking Time: 2-2¼ hours*

**50g/2 oz streaky bacon, rinds removed, and chopped**
**1 tbsp vegetable oil**
**450g/1 lb rabbit, thawed and diced**
**1 medium onion, peeled and chopped**
**1 medium carrot, peeled and sliced**
**½ green pepper, deseeded and diced**
**1 level tsp dried mixed herbs**
**600ml/1 pt chicken stock**

**350g/12 oz frozen flaky or puff pastry, thawed**
**1 medium egg, lightly beaten for the glaze**

**1 level tbsp cornflour**
**3 tbsp milk**
**Salt and pepper**

1.  Lightly fry the bacon and oil in a large pan. Add the rabbit, onion, carrot, green pepper, herbs and stock. Bring to the boil and reduce heat to simmer for 1 hour or until the rabbit is tender.

2.  Meanwhile, on a floured board roll out the pastry to 2.5cm/1 inch larger than a 1.2 litre/2 pt pie dish. Cut a 5mm/¼ inch strip of pastry from the rolled-out piece. Cover with a piece of greaseproof paper to prevent it drying out.

3.  When the rabbit is cooked, mix together the cornflour and milk. Pour into the pan and bring to the boil. Season to taste.

4.  Spoon the mixture into the pie dish and place a pie funnel in the centre.

5.  Dampen the edge of the dish with a little egg and place the pastry strip around the dish. Brush with egg and place the large piece of pastry over the top. Press down

44

the edges with a fork to make a pattern. Glaze the top
with beaten egg. Make a hole in the top of the pastry
where the pie funnel is placed.

6.   Bake in a preheated oven at 180°C for 15-25 minutes or
     until the pastry is risen and golden brown.

## Quiche Lorraine

By using Gruyère cheese, the really French flavour is
achieved. However, Cheddar cheese can be used as a
substitute.

*Serves 6-8*

*Preparation and Cooking Time: 70-90 minutes*

**225g/8 oz frozen shortcrust pastry, thawed**
**75g/3 oz streaky bacon, rinds removed, and chopped**
**150g/6 oz Gruyère cheese, grated**
**3 medium egg yolks**
**300ml/½ pint milk**
**Salt and pepper**
**3 medium egg whites**

1.   On a floured board, roll out the dough if necessary and
     line a 21cm/8½ inch flan case.

2.   In a bowl, mix together the bacon, cheese, egg yolks,
     milk and salt and pepper to taste.

3.   In a separate bowl, whisk the egg whites until stiff and
     gently fold into the cheese mixture. Pour into the flan
     case.

4.   Bake in a preheated oven at 160°C for 50-65 minutes.
     Once the top has turned a pale brown, lightly cover with
     a piece of foil to slow down the browning and to allow
     the pastry to finish cooking.

# Moussaka

This recipe can be cooked from cold but you may need to add about 5-10 minutes to the cooking time.

If you don't like aubergine, substitute with cooked, sliced potatoes.

*Serves 4*

*Preparation and Cooking Time: 1-1¼ hours*

**Aubergine, with a total weight of 675g/1½ lb, cut into thin slices**
**Salt and pepper**

**6-8 tbsp olive or vegetable oil**
**1 large onion, peeled and chopped**
**2 cloves garlic, crushed**
**450g/1 lb minced lamb**
**3 tbsp tomato purée**
**1 tsp mixed dried herbs**
**285ml/½ pint lamb or meat stock**

*Sauce*
**25g/1 oz butter or margarine**
**25g/1 oz flour**
**285ml/½ pint milk**
**1 medium egg, lightly beaten**

1. Sprinkle the aubergine with salt and stand for 30 minutes. Rinse in cold water and pat dry.

2. Meanwhile, heat 3 tablespoons oil in a pan. Gently fry the onion and garlic until soft.

3. Stir in the lamb and fry until sealed and brown. Add the tomato purée, herbs and stock. Season to taste. Bring to the boil, cover and simmer for about 30 minutes or until the meat is tender and most of the liquid has been absorbed.

4. Using the remaining oil, fry the aubergine until browned. Layer the aubergine and the meat in a dish measuring 17.5 × 20.5cm/7 × 9 inches, finishing with a layer of aubergine.

5.   Melt the butter in a pan, stir in the flour until the butter is absorbed. Gradually stir in the milk. When thick, beat in the egg and season to taste.

6.   Pour the sauce over the aubergine and bake in a preheated oven at 170°C for 25-35 minutes or until the top is browned.


## Sausage, Onion and Tomato Casserole

This recipe can be cooked from cold but you may need to add about 5-10 minutes to the cooking time.
   If preferred, the tomatoes can be substituted with stock.

*Serves 4*

*Preparation and Cooking Time: 1½-1¾ hours*

**2 tbsp vegetable oil**
**1 large onion, peeled and sliced**
**8 thick sausages, chopped in half**
**400g/14 oz can, chopped tomatoes with herbs**
**1 beef stock cube, crumbled**
**2 tbsp tomato sauce**
**Salt and pepper**

1.   Heat the oil in a pan and gently fry the onion until soft. Remove the onion and add the sausages. Fry until browned on all sides.

2.   Add the onion, tomatoes, beef stock cube, tomato sauce and salt and pepper to taste. Bring to the boil, cover and simmer for 5-10 minutes.

3.   Pour into a 1.2 litre/2 pt casserole dish, cover and cook in a preheated oven at 150°C for 1-1¼ hours or until the sausages are cooked through.

# Sweet and Sour Chicken

This recipe can be cooked from cold but you may need to add about 5-10 minutes to the cooking time.

*Serves 4*

*Preparation and Cooking Time: 1¾-2 hours*

25g/1 oz butter or margarine
2 tsp vegetable oil
4 chicken legs with a total weight of 1kg/2¼ lb
1 medium onion, peeled and chopped
½ red pepper, deseeded and chopped
½ green pepper, deseeded and chopped
2 cloves garlic, peeled and crushed
50g/2 oz mushrooms, chopped
25g/1 oz plain flour
425ml/¾ pt chicken stock
1 tsp mixed dried herbs
1 level tbsp desiccated coconut
2 tbsp white wine vinegar
1 tbsp soy sauce
1 rounded tbsp marmalade
50g/2 oz soft brown sugar
Salt and pepper

1.  Heat the butter and oil in a pan. Brown the chicken on both sides. Remove and place into a deep casserole dish.

2.  Stir the onion, peppers, garlic and mushrooms into the pan. Gently cook until the onion is soft.

3.  Stir in the flour, and gradually add the stock. Add the herbs, coconut, vinegar, soy sauce, marmalade and sugar. Bring to the boil, season to taste and pour over the chicken.

4.  Cover and cook in a preheated oven at 160°C for 1¼-1½ hours or until the juices run clear when the chicken is pierced with a sharp knife.

# Guard of Honour

This recipe can be cooked from cold but you may need to add about 5-10 minutes to the cooking time.

This looks splendid to serve, is fairly inexpensive to buy and is very simple to prepare and cook. Ask the butcher to prepare the guard of honour. It also tastes good served cold.

*Serves 4*

*Preparation and Cooking Time: 1¾-2½ hours*

**25g/1 oz butter**
**1 small onion, finely chopped**
**25g/1 oz walnuts, chopped**
**50g/2 oz dried apricots, chopped**
**2 tbsp parsley, finely chopped**
**50g/2 oz fresh white breadcrumbs**
**Grated rind and juice of one orange**
**Salt and pepper**
**2 whole best end neck of lamb with a total weight of**
  **1.75kg/3½ lb, prepared into a guard of honour**

1. Melt the butter in a pan and fry the onion until soft.

2. Mix the butter and onion with the walnuts, apricots, parsley, breadcrumbs, orange rind and juice. Season to taste. Fill centre of lamb with the stuffing.

3. Place the stuffed lamb into a roasting pan and cover with foil.

4. Roast in a preheated oven at 170°C for 1¾-2 hours or until cooked to the desired degree. Remove the foil 15 minutes before the end of the cooking time to colour the stuffing.

# Steak and Kidney Pie

Using wine as a marinade improves the tenderness of the meat. For a different flavour, beer can be used as a substitute. Should no marinade be used, the cooking time may be longer.

*Serves 4*

*Preparation and Cooking Time: 2-2½ hours plus marinating*

**675g/1½ lb braising steak, trimmed and cut into cubes**
**140ml/¼ pt red wine**
**160g/6 oz kidneys, cored and sliced**
**50g/2 oz plain flour, seasoned with salt and pepper**
**3 tbsp vegetable oil**
**1 onion, peeled and chopped**
**285ml/½ pt beef stock**
**1 tsp dried chopped herbs**
**Salt and pepper**

**350g/12 oz frozen flaky or puff pastry, thawed**
**1 egg, beaten, for the glaze**

1. Place the meat in a bowl and pour the wine over. Marinate overnight or for at least 2 hours in a refrigerator. Drain and discard the wine marinade.

2. Toss the meat and kidneys in the seasoned flour.

3. Heat the oil in a pan and lightly cook the onion. Remove the onion and add the meat mixture. Fry to brown and seal for 5-10 minutes, stirring occasionally to avoid sticking. Stir in the onion, stock and herbs. Bring to the boil, cover, then simmer for 45-60 minutes or until the meat is cooked. Stir occasionally to check that the meat is not sticking to the base of the pan.

4. Meanwhile, on a floured board roll out the pastry to 2.5cm/1 inch larger than a 1.2 litre/2 pt pie dish. Cut a 5mm/¼ inch strip of pastry from the rolled-out piece. Cover with a piece of greaseproof paper to prevent it drying out.

5. When the meat is cooked, season to taste and spoon the mixture into the pie dish and place a pie funnel in the centre.

6. Dampen the edge of the dish with a little egg and place the pastry strip around the dish. Brush with egg and place the large piece of pastry over the top. Press down the edges with a fork to make a pattern. Brush the top with beaten egg. Make a hole in the top of the pastry where the pie funnel is placed.

7. Bake in a preheated oven at 180°C for 15-25 minutes or until the pastry is risen and golden brown.

## Lamb Hotpot

This recipe can be cooked from cold but you may need to add about 5-10 minutes to the cooking time.
  Pork chops can be used as a substitute for lamb.

*Serves 4*

*Preparation and Cooking Time: 1¾-2¼ hours*

**4 lamb chops with a total weight of 500g/1 lb 2 oz**
**2 large onions, peeled and sliced**
**2 carrots, peeled and sliced**
**2 large potatoes, peeled and sliced**
**Salt and pepper**
**500ml/1 pt hot meat or vegetable stock**
**Vegetable oil for brushing**

1. In a 2 litre/4 pt casserole dish, layer the chops, vegetables and salt and pepper to taste. Finish with a top layer of potatoes.

2. Pour the hot stock over and brush the potato topping with oil.

3. Cover the casserole with the lid and cook in a preheated oven at 150°C for 1¾-2 hours or until the meat is tender.

# Shepherd's Pie

This recipe can be cooked from cold but you may need to add about 5-10 minutes to the cooking time.

For a change, substitute the minced meat with minced turkey.

*Serves 4*

*Preparation and Cooking Time: 1-1¼ hours*

**675g/1½ lb potatoes, peeled and cut into pieces**
**Salt and pepper**
**25g/1 oz butter**
**4 tbsp milk**
**1 onion, peeled and chopped**
**25g/1 oz lard or dripping**
**350g/12 oz minced beef or lamb**
**100g/4 oz mushrooms, chopped**
**400g/14 oz can chopped tomatoes with herbs**
**1 meat stock cube, crumbled**
**1 tsp tomato sauce**

1.  In a pan place the potatoes with sufficient water to cover. Add a pinch of salt. Cover with a lid and boil for about 20-25 minutes until cooked. Mash with the butter and milk, and season to taste.

2.  Meanwhile, place the onion and lard in a pan and gently fry until soft. Add the meat and cook until browned.

3.  Add the mushrooms and stir in the canned tomatoes, stock cube, tomato sauce and salt and pepper to taste. Bring to the boil and simmer for 20-25 minutes.

4.  Spoon the meat into 850ml-1.2 litre/1½-2 pt ovenproof dish. Spread the mashed potatoes over the meat and cook in a preheated oven at 170°C for 30-40 minutes or until browned.

# Roast Beef

Beef must always be stored in a refrigerator, on a plate or dish, covered and not touching any other cooked or uncooked meats. If frozen, it must be completely thawed before use.

This recipe can be cooked from cold but you may need to add about 5-10 minutes to the cooking time.

Roast for about 50-60 minutes per kilo plus an extra 40 minutes or for 25-30 minutes per pound plus an extra 20 minutes.

Whether well done, medium or rare depends upon your taste. Well done is relatively easy to achieve but for other tastes it is possibly better to use a roasting thermometer inserted into the meat. A guide to the degree of cooking without a thermometer:

Well done – very brown with no bloody juices;

Medium – brown meat with bloody juices;

Rare – bloody when hot.

After cooking, stand for 10 minutes before carving.

*Serves 8-10*

*Preparation and Cooking Time: 2½-3 hours*

**1 topside beef weighing 2.3kg/5 lb**
**Salt and pepper**
**4 tbsp vegetable oil**

1. Wipe the joint with a damp cloth. Place on a trivet in a roasting tin, season to taste and rub with oil.

2. Roast in a preheated oven at 170°C for 2¼-2¾ hours or until the meat is cooked to the desired degree. Turn over halfway through cooking.

3. Remove the meat and stand for 10 minutes before carving.

# Lasagne

This recipe can be cooked from cold but you may need to add about 5-10 minutes to the cooking time.

To make the recipe for a vegetarian, substitute the meat with the same quantity of vegetables such as courgettes, additional sweet pepper, carrots and tomatoes, and replace the meat stock with vegetable stock.

*Serves 4*

*Preparation and Cooking Time: 1½-2 hours*

**6 sheets green lasagne**

*Filling*
**4 streaky bacon rashers, rinds removed, and chopped**
**1 medium onion, peeled and finely chopped**
**50g/2 oz mushrooms, chopped**
**Small green pepper, core removed, deseeded and diced**
**2 garlic cloves, crushed**
**450g/1 lb minced meat**
**140ml/¼ pt meat stock**
**140ml/¼ pt can chopped tomatoes**
**½ level tsp dried oregano**
**½ level tsp dried basil**
**Salt and pepper**

*Topping*
**40g/1½ oz butter or margarine**
**40g/1½ oz plain flour**
**425ml/¾ pt milk**
**50g/2 oz Parmesan or Cheddar cheese, grated**

1.  Place the lasagne in a pan of boiling water and boil for 10-15 minutes or until just tender. Drain, place in a bowl of cold water and separate any sheets under the water should they have stuck together. Set aside until required.

2.  Lightly fry the bacon in a pan and add the onion, mushrooms, pepper and garlic. Gently cook for 5 minutes. Stir in the meat and lightly brown, then add the stock, tomatoes and herbs. Season to taste. Bring to

the boil and then simmer for 20 minutes or until cooked.

3.   Melt the butter in a pan, stir in the flour. Gradually add the milk, stirring all the while. Season to taste.

4.   In a 17.5 × 20.5cm/7 × 9 inch ovenproof dish, spoon over a layer of meat, then half the drained lasagne. Repeat and then pour over the sauce.

5.   Sprinkle with cheese and bake in a preheated oven at 170°C for 15-25 minutes or until the top is golden brown and bubbling.

## Pork Chop Casserole

This recipe can be cooked from cold but you may need to add about 5-10 minutes to the cooking time. Lamb chops can be used as a substitute for the pork chops.

*Serves 4*

*Preparation and Cooking Time: 1½-2 hours*

**25g/1 oz butter or margarine**
**2 tsp vegetable oil**
**4 pork chops, with a total weight of 675g/1½ lb**
**1 large carrot, peeled and sliced**
**1 large onion, peeled and sliced**
**1 stick of celery, chopped**
**25g/1 oz plain flour**
**285ml/½ pt lamb or beef stock**
**Salt and pepper**
**½ tsp gravy browning**

1.   Melt the butter and oil in a pan and fry the chops on both sides to seal and brown. Place in a casserole dish.

2.   Stir in the carrot, onion and celery. Cook gently until the onion is soft. Stir in the flour and gradually add the stock. Bring to the boil and season to taste, add the gravy browning.

3.   Pour the vegetables and stock over the chops. Cover and cook in a preheated oven at 160°C for 1¼-1½ hours or until the chops are tender.

# Toad in the Hole

I always make my batter at least 1-2 hours in advance and then leave it to stand.

For a change, lamb chops can be used to substitute the sausages.

*Serves 4*

*Preparation and Cooking Time: 45-60 minutes*

**5 tbsp vegetable oil**
**450g/1 lb thick sausages**
**100g/4 oz plain flour**
**Pinch salt**
**1 medium egg**
**140ml/¼ pt milk and 140ml/¼ pt water mixed together**

1.  Place the oil and sausages in a 17.5 × 20.5cm/7 × 9 inch roasting pan and cook in a preheated oven at 190°C for 15-20 minutes or until the sausages are partly browned.

2.  Place the flour and salt in a bowl and make a well in the centre. Place the egg, milk and water in the centre and gradually stir the liquid into the flour. Once incorporated, beat well until smooth.

3.  Turn the sausages over and pour the batter over them. Increase the oven temperature to 210°C and cook for 20-30 minutes or until the batter is risen and brown.

# Roast Chicken

This recipe can be cooked from cold but you may need to add about 5-10 minutes to the cooking time.

Chicken should always be stored in a refrigerator, on a plate or dish, covered and not touching any other cooked or uncooked meat. If frozen, it must be completely thawed before use. Stuffing the cavity is not advised (as there could be a chance that the meat around the stuffing is not sufficiently cooked) although the neck area can be stuffed if desired.

Regardless of size, roast for about 40 minutes per kilo plus an extra 40 minutes or for 20 minutes per pound plus an extra 20 minutes.

The chicken is cooked when the thickest part, the thigh, is pierced and the juices run clear.

After cooking, stand for 10 minutes before carving.

*Serves 6-8*

*Cooking and Preparation Time: 2¼-2¾ hours*

**1 chicken weighing 2.4kg/5½ lb**
**Salt and pepper**
**4 streaky bacon rashers**

1. Remove the neck and any giblets from inside the chicken. Wipe the outside and inside with a damp cloth.

2. Place on a trivet in a roasting tin, season to taste and cover the breast with the bacon. Roast in a preheated oven at 180°C for 2-2½ hours or until the juices run clear when a skewer is inserted into the thighs.

3. Remove the bacon and allow to stand for 10 minutes before carving.

# Duck Breasts with Wine Sauce

This recipe can be cooked from cold but you may need to add about 5-10 minutes to the cooking time.

The sauce is slightly sharp to complement the richness of the duck. I like to blend it in a blender for a smoother consistency but if preferred it can be served without blending.

*Serves 4*

*Preparation and Cooking Time: 30-40 minutes*

**4 duck breast fillets with a total weight of 675g/1½ lb**

*Sauce*
**2 tbsp olive or vegetable oil**
**1 medium onion, peeled and finely chopped**
**2 button mushrooms, chopped**
**2 cloves garlic, crushed**
**1 level tbsp plain flour**
**140ml/¼ pt red wine**
**140ml/¼ pt chicken stock**
**1 tsp castor sugar**
**1 tsp soy sauce**
**Salt and pepper**

1.  Place the duck in a non-stick frying pan and fry on both sides to seal and lightly brown. Place in a roasting tin, meat side down, and roast in a preheated oven at 170°C for 15-20 minutes or until the skin is crisp and the meat, when pierced, is slightly pink.

2.  Meanwhile in a pan, heat the oil and gently cook the onion, mushrooms and garlic until soft.

3.  Stir in the flour and cook for a minute, stirring all the time. Gradually stir in the wine and stock. Stir in the sugar, soy sauce and season to taste. Bring to the boil and cook for a minute or two. Pass through a blender, check seasoning and adjust if desired.

4.  Either arrange the duck breasts on a plate and pour the sauce around or serve the sauce separately.

# Pork in Cider

This recipe can be cooked from cold but you may need to add about 5-10 minutes to the cooking time.

Although less usual, veal could be used instead of pork.

*Serves 4*

*Preparation and Cooking Time: 1¾-2 hours*

**50g/2 oz butter or margarine**
**2 tsp vegetable oil**
**1 medium onion, peeled and chopped**
**½ red pepper, deseeded and diced**
**1 stick celery, finely chopped**
**550g/1¼ lb pork, diced**
**25g/1 oz plain flour, seasoned with salt and pepper**
**285ml/½ pt strong dry cider**
**140ml/¼ pt chicken stock**
**1 level tsp dried marjoram**
**Salt and pepper**
**1 dessert apple, washed, cored and cut into thick slices**

1.  Melt the butter and oil in a pan. Stir in the onion, pepper and celery. Gently cook the vegetables until softened.

2.  Toss the meat in the flour and stir into the vegetables. Cook until sealed and lightly browned.

3.  Gradually add the cider and stock and bring to the boil. Add the marjoram and season to taste. Boil for about 2 minutes.

4.  Arrange the apple in the base of a casserole dish and spoon the pork mixture over. Cover and cook in a preheated oven at 160°C for 1¼-1½ hours or until the pork is tender.

# Goulash

This recipe can be cooked from cold but you may need to add about 5-10 minutes to the cooking time. Using wine as a marinade improves the tenderness of meat. If you don't use a marinade, the cooking time may be longer.

*Serves 4*

*Preparation and Cooking Time: 2½-2¾ hours plus marinating*

675g/1½ lb braising steak, trimmed and cut into cubes
140ml/¼ pt red wine
40g/1½ oz plain flour, seasoned with salt and pepper
2 tbsp vegetable oil
1 medium onion, peeled and chopped
550ml/1 pt beef stock
196g/7 oz can plum tomatoes with juice, chopped
2 level tbsp tomato purée
1 level tsp dried marjoram
1 level tbsp paprika powder
2 level tsp castor sugar
Salt and pepper
75ml/2½ fl oz soured cream

1.  Place the meat in a bowl and pour the wine over. Marinate overnight, or for at least 2 hours, in a refrigerator. Drain and discard the wine marinade. Toss the meat in the seasoned flour.

2.  Heat the oil in a pan and gently cook the onion until soft. Remove from the heat, and add the meat mixture. Fry to lightly brown and seal for 5-10 minutes, stirring occasionally to avoid sticking.

3.  Gradually stir in the stock, tomatoes with the juice and the purée, bring to the boil. Stir in the marjoram, paprika and sugar. Season to taste.

4.  Spoon into a casserole dish, cover and cook in a preheated oven at 150°C for 2-2¼ hours or until the meat is tender. Prior to serving, stir in the soured cream.

# Stewed Steak with Herb Dumplings

This recipe can be cooked from cold but you may need to add about 5-10 minutes to the cooking time. Should you prefer plain dumplings, you can leave the herbs out.

*Serves 4*

*Preparation and Cooking Time: 2¾-3 hours*

**550g/1¼ lb braising steak, trimmed and cubed**
**25g/1 oz plain flour, seasoned with salt and pepper**
**3 tbsp vegetable oil**
**1 carrot, peeled and sliced**
**1 medium onion, peeled and chopped**
**50g/2 oz mushrooms, chopped**
**½ green pepper, deseeded and diced**
**196g/7 oz can plum tomatoes with juice, chopped**
**550ml/1 pt beef stock**
**Salt and pepper**

*Dumplings*
**100g/4 oz self raising flour**
**50g/2 oz shredded suet**
**2 level tsp dried mixed herbs**
**8-9 tbsp cold water**

1.  Toss the meat in the seasoned flour.
2.  Heat the oil in a pan and gently cook the carrot, onion, mushrooms and green pepper until softened. Add the meat mixture. Fry to lightly brown and seal for 5-10 minutes, stirring occasionally to avoid sticking. Gradually stir in the tomatoes with the juice and the stock, bring to the boil. Season to taste.
3.  Spoon into a casserole dish, cover and cook in a preheated oven at 150°C for 1½ hours.
4.  Meanwhile, make the dumplings. Mix together the flour, suet and herbs. Season to taste. Stir in the water and, when thoroughly mixed, use your hands to form into ten balls. Set aside, covered, until needed.
5.  Add the dumplings to the casserole, cover and cook for a further 45-60 minutes or until the meat is tender.

# Meat Balls in Tomato Sauce

This recipe can be cooked from cold but you may need to add about 5-10 minutes to the cooking time.

Any mince can be used instead of the beef. For a less strong tomato sauce, use a small can of tomatoes and 550ml/1 pt stock.

*Serves 4*

*Preparation and Cooking Time: 1¼-1½ hours*

**450g/1 lb minced beef**
**1 level tsp mixed dried herbs**
**1 medium onion, peeled and finely chopped**
**½ medium egg, lightly beaten**
**Salt and pepper**
**25g/1 oz plain flour, seasoned with salt and pepper**
**4 tbsp vegetable oil**

*Sauce*
**25g/1 oz butter or margarine**
**25g/1 oz plain flour**
**400g/14 oz can chopped tomatoes with juice**
**285ml/½ pt meat stock**
**1 level tsp dried mixed herbs**
**1 tbsp tomato sauce or purée**

1. Using your hands, mix together the beef, herbs, onion, egg and salt and pepper to taste.

2. Form into 16 balls and roll in the seasoned flour. Heat the oil and fry the balls until evenly browned, turning as required. Place the balls in a casserole dish.

3. To make the sauce: Melt the butter in a pan and stir in the flour. Gradually add the tomatoes, juice, and stock. Bring to the boil, stirring all the time, and add the herbs and tomato sauce. Season to taste.

4. Pour the sauce over the meatballs, cover and bake in a preheated oven at 160°C for 45-55 minutes or until the meatballs are cooked through.

# Roast Guinea Fowl

This recipe can be cooked from cold but you may need to add about 5-10 minutes to the cooking time.

This fowl is of the turkey family but the flavour is slightly gamey and somewhat similar to pheasant. It is cooked like chicken although it is advisable to keep it moist by covering the breast with bacon as it can tend to dry out.

Guinea fowl should always be stored in a refrigerator, on a plate or dish, covered and not touching any other cooked or uncooked meat. If frozen, it must be completely thawed before use. Stuffing the cavity is not advised (as there could be a chance that the meat around the stuffing is not sufficiently cooked) although the neck area can be stuffed if desired.

Regardless of size, roast for about 40 minutes per kilo plus an extra 40 minutes or for 20 minutes per pound plus an extra 20 minutes.

The guinea fowl is cooked when the thickest part, the thigh, is pierced and the juices run clear.

After cooking, stand for 10 minutes before carving.

*Serves 2-3*

*Preparation and Cooking Time: 1¼-1½ hours*

**1 guinea fowl weighing 1.1kg/2 lb**
**Salt and pepper**
**3 streaky bacon rashers**

1.  Remove the neck and any giblets from inside the fowl. Wipe the outside and inside with a damp cloth.

2.  Place on a trivet in a roasting tin, season to taste and cover the breast with the bacon. Roast in a preheated oven at 160°C for 55-65 minutes or until the juices run clear when a skewer is inserted into the thighs.

3.  Remove the bacon and allow to stand for 10 minutes before carving.

# Spatchcock

This recipe can be cooked from cold but you may need to add about 5-10 minutes to the cooking time.

Spatchcock is a method of cooking small poultry or game birds by splitting them down the back and grilling or oven roasting. Nowadays most supermarkets and butchers sell prepared birds but should you wish to prepare them yourself it is relatively easy. Place the bird breast side down on a board and, using scissors, cut along one side of the backbone. Then cut through the other side of the backbone and remove the bone. Turn the bird over and gently pull the legs and wings to each side of the breast. Using two skewers, push each diagonally through a leg, then through the breast and finally through the wing.

*Serves 2-4*

*Preparation and Cooking Time: 1-1¼ hours*

**2 spatchcock of chicken with a total weight of 900g/2 lb**
**Vegetable oil for brushing**
**2 tbsp mixed fresh herbs, including parsley, sage,**
**    thyme and rosemary, chopped or 1 tbsp of dried**
**    mixed herbs**

1.   Brush or rub the oil over the breast, legs and wings. Rub in the herbs.

2.   Place the spatchcocks breast side up in a roasting tin and roast in a preheated oven at 170°C for 40-50 minutes or until the juices run clear when a skewer is inserted into the thighs.

3.   Stand for 5 minutes before removing the skewers and serving.

# Cornish Pasties

Originating in Cornwall, large boat-shaped pasties made a filling 'packed lunch' for tin miners and farm workers.

*Serves 4*

*Preparation and Cooking Time: 1½-1¾ hours*

**2 medium potatoes, peeled and cut into 1cm/½ inch cubes**
**250g/8 oz lean braising steak, cut into 1cm/½ inch cubes**
**2 onions, peeled and finely chopped**
**Salt and pepper**
**500g/1 lb 2 oz frozen shortcrust pastry, thawed**
**Flour for rolling out**
**Lightly beaten egg**

1.  Place the potatoes in a pan of cold water. Bring to the boil and boil for 5 minutes. Drain and cool.

2.  Combine the potatoes with the meat, onion, salt and pepper to taste.

3.  Divide the pastry into four. Roll out on a lightly floured board to form four circles of approximately 20cm/8 inch diameter.

4.  Divide the meat mixture between the pastry rounds. Dampen the edges with a little cold water and draw together to form a seam over the top. Crimp the edges and brush with beaten egg. Place onto a greased baking sheet.

5.  Bake in a preheated oven at 180°C for 15 minutes, reduce to 140°C and bake for a further 50-60 minutes or until the pastry is golden brown and the filling cooked.

# Pork Cobbler

This recipe can be cooked from cold but you may need to add about 5-10 minutes to the cooking time.

The scone topping makes a change to pastry. To add more interest, add a teaspoon of mixed dried herbs to the scone mixture before adding the milk.

*Serves 4*

*Preparation and Cooking Time: 2-2¼ hours*

**550g/1¼ lb pork, diced**
**25g/1 oz plain flour, seasoned with salt and pepper**
**50g/2 oz butter or margarine**
**1 medium onion, peeled and chopped**
**1 carrot, peeled and diced**
**2 sticks celery, washed and finely chopped**
**½ green pepper, deseeded and diced**
**2 mushrooms, chopped**
**1 tsp dried tarragon**
**425ml/¾ pt meat stock**

*Topping*
**225g/8 oz plain flour**
**Pinch salt**
**50g/2 oz butter or margarine**
**7-8 tbsp milk**

1. Toss the meat in the seasoned flour.

2. Melt the butter in a pan and stir in the onion, carrot, celery, green pepper, mushrooms and tarragon. Gently fry until the vegetables have softened.

3. Stir in the meat and fry until sealed and lightly browned. Add the stock and bring to the boil. Spoon into a casserole dish, cover and cook in a preheated oven at 160°C for 1-1¼ hours or until the meat is tender.

4. Meanwhile, make the topping. Sieve together the flour and salt. Rub in the butter until the mixture looks like fine breadcrumbs. Add sufficient milk to make the pastry into a dough.

5.  On a floured board, roll out the pastry to a thickness of about 1cm/½ inch and cut out 12 scones using a 5cm/ 2 inch cutter.

6.  Place the scones on top of the cooked meat, overlapping in a circle around the edge of the casserole. Bake, uncovered, at 170°C for 20-30 minutes or until risen and brown.

## Spare Ribs

This recipe can be cooked from cold but you may need to add about 5-10 minutes to the cooking time.

*Serves 4*

*Preparation and Cooking Time: 1¾-2 hours*

**2 tbsp vegetable oil**
**2 onions, peeled and finely chopped**
**2 garlic cloves, peeled and finely chopped**
**2 tbsp tomato purée**
**2 tbsp malt vinegar**
**½ tsp dried thyme**
**½ tsp chilli powder**
**2 tbsp honey**
**125ml/¼ pt stock**
**Salt and pepper**
**1kg/2 lb 4 oz pork spare ribs**

1.  Heat the oil in a pan, add the onions and cook until softened. Stir in the garlic, purée, vinegar, thyme, chilli powder, honey, stock, and salt and pepper to taste. Cook gently for 10-15 minutes or until the onion is cooked through.

2.  Place the spare ribs into a roasting pan and lightly coat with some of the sauce.

3.  Roast in a preheated oven at 170°C for 30 minutes. Pour over the remaining sauce and roast for a further 1-1¼ hours or until the ribs are tender. Baste from time to time during roasting.

# Glazed Gammon

This recipe can be cooked from cold but you may need to add about 5-10 minutes to the cooking time.

*Serves 4*

*Preparation time: 15 minutes*

*Cooking time: Allow 30 minutes per 450g/1 lb and 30 minutes extra.*

**1 gammon joint**

*Glaze*
**1 tbsp thick cut marmalade**
**15g/½ oz melted butter**
**1 tsp dried mustard**

1.  Wrap the joint with foil and place into a roasting tin.

2.  Roast in a preheated oven at 170°C for 30 minutes per 450g/lb and 30 minutes extra.

3.  Mix together the marmalade, butter and mustard.

4.  Remove the gammon skin 30 minutes before the end of cooking and brush the glaze over the fat. Return to the oven to complete the cooking time.

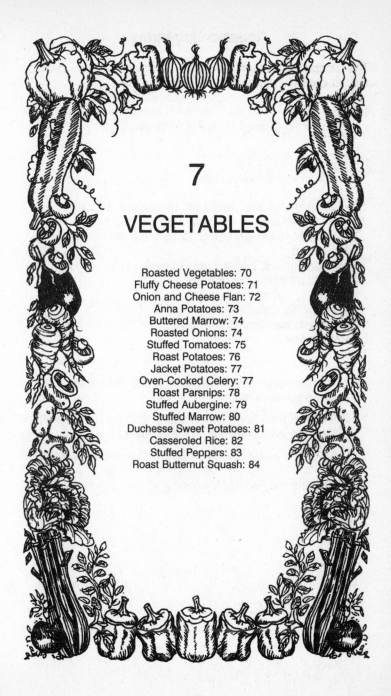

# 7

# VEGETABLES

# Roasted Vegetables

This recipe can be cooked from cold but you may need to add about 5-10 minutes to the cooking time.

Although the recipe includes specific vegetables, you can use any combination you like. If I'm serving six, I often add a can of drained sweetcorn at the halfway stage.

*Serves 4*

*Preparation and Cooking Time: 1-1¼ hours*

**1 yellow pepper, top removed, deseeded and sliced**
**225g/8 oz aubergine, top removed, and sliced**
**2 courgettes, total weight of 225g/8 oz, stems removed,**
    **and sliced**
**225g/8 oz onions, peeled and sliced**
**100g/4 oz mushrooms, sliced**
**2 tomatoes, cut into quarters**
**1 clove garlic, crushed**
**1 tbsp fresh rosemary, chopped**
**Salt and pepper**
**125ml/4 fl oz vegetable oil**

1.  Toss together the vegetables, garlic, rosemary and salt and pepper to taste.

2.  Place in a roasting pan measuring 17.5 × 20.5cm/7 × 9 inches and pour half of the oil over.

3.  Bake in a preheated oven at 190°C for 45-60 minutes or until the vegetables are cooked. Halfway through roasting, turn the vegetables over and pour the remaining oil over .

# Fluffy Cheese Potatoes

This recipe can be cooked from cold but you may need to add about 5-10 minutes to the cooking time.

*Serves 4*

*Preparation and Cooking Time: 2-2¼ hours*

**4 baking potatoes with a total weight of 900g/2 lb,
     scrubbed and pricked
Vegetable cooking oil
40g/1½ oz butter or margarine
2 medium egg yolks
4 tbsp double cream
Salt and pepper
2 medium egg whites
50g/2 oz Parmesan or Cheddar cheese**

1.   Rub each potato in oil and place in the oven on a
     baking sheet.

2.   Bake in a preheated oven at 170°C for 1¼-1½ hours or
     until the potatoes are cooked.

3.   Remove from the oven and slice the top off each potato
     lengthways. Scoop out the flesh into a bowl.

4.   Beat the butter, egg yolks, cream and salt and pepper
     to taste into the flesh.

5.   In a separate bowl, whisk the egg whites until stiff and
     gently fold into the potato mixture. Return the filling to
     the potato skins. Sprinkle the grated cheese over.

6.   Return to the oven and bake for a further 20-30 minutes
     or until the cheese has melted and has turned brown.

# Onion and Cheese Flan

The flan can be served hot or cold as a main dish or for a party. Cheddar cheese can be used as a substitute for the Parmesan.

*Serves 4-6*

*Preparation and Cooking Time: 1-1½ hours*

**225g/8 oz frozen shortcrust pastry, thawed**
**50g/2 oz butter**
**1 tsp cooking oil**
**450g/1 lb onions, peeled and thinly sliced**
**2 medium eggs**
**140ml/¼ pt double cream**
**140ml/¼ pt milk**
**25g/1 oz Parmesan cheese, finely grated**
**Salt and pepper**

1. On a floured board, roll out the pastry and line a 21cm/8½ inch flan case. Place in a refrigerator.

2. Place the butter and oil in a frying pan, add the onions and gently cook for about 15-20 minutes until soft and lightly browned.

3. Beat together the eggs, cream and milk in a bowl. Stir in the cheese and onions and season to taste.

4. Pour into the pastry case and bake in a preheated oven at 170°C for 25 minutes. Cover the top lightly with a piece of foil to slow down the browning and to allow the pastry to finish cooking.

5. Bake for a further 15-20 minutes or until the pastry is cooked, the top brown and the mixture firm to the touch.

# Anna Potatoes

This recipe can be cooked from cold but you may need to add about 5-10 minutes to the cooking time.

If preferred use milk instead of cream. For a potato and onion recipe, place layers of thinly sliced onions between the potato layers but always finish with a layer of potatoes.

*Serves 4*

*Preparation and Cooking Time: 55-70 minutes*

**675g/1½ lb potatoes, peeled and thinly sliced**
**Salt and pepper**
**140ml/¼ pt single cream**
**50g/2 oz butter or margarine**

1.  In a buttered 1.2 litre/2 pt soufflé dish arrange layers of potato. Season to taste, pour over the cream and dot with butter.

2.  Cover and bake in a preheated oven at 170°C for 30 minutes. Remove the cover and continue to cook for 15-20 minutes or until the top is crisp, and the potatoes are cooked and have absorbed the cream.

# Buttered Marrow

This recipe can be cooked from cold but you may need to add about 5-10 minutes to the cooking time.

*Serves 3-4*

*Preparation and Cooking Time: 40-50 minutes*

**1 × 1.2kg/2½ lb marrow, peeled, cut into 2.5cm/1 inch slices, seeds removed, and quartered**
**50g/2 oz butter**
**Salt and pepper**

1.  Prepare the marrow and place in a shallow casserole dish. Place knobs of butter over the marrow and season to taste.

2.  Cover and cook in a preheated oven at 170°C for 30-40 minutes or until the marrow is tender. Drain and serve if desired with a white or cheese sauce.

# Roasted Onions

This recipe can be cooked from cold but you may need to add about 5-10 minutes to the cooking time.
  Serve as a vegetable for inside or outside dining.

*Serves 4*

*Preparation and Cooking Time: 1¼-1½ hours*

**4 large onions with a total weight of 900g/2 lb, unpeeled, washed**

1.  On the sides where the roots have been removed, stand the onions in a shallow foil-lined dish.

2.  Bake in a preheated oven at 170°C for 1-1¼ hours or until the onions are tender.

3.  Remove the skins and serve.

# Stuffed Tomatoes

This recipe can be cooked from cold but you may need to add about 5-10 minutes to the cooking time.

Using a shop-bought filling gives a very strong flavour. However, you can create your own filling with fresh breadcrumbs and the herbs of your choice.

When scooping out the flesh, I find that using a grapefruit knife makes the process easier.

*Serves 4*

*Preparation and Cooking Time: ¾-1 hour*

**4 large tomatoes with a total weight of 800g/1¾ lb**
**3 level tbsp sage and onion stuffing**
**Salt and pepper**

1.  Cut the top off each tomato, remove the flesh and finely chop. Keep the tomato tops.

2.  Mix the flesh with the stuffing and season to taste. Return the filling to the tomatoes.

3.  Place the tomatoes in a shallow, buttered dish and lightly cover with greaseproof paper. Bake in a pre-heated oven at 170°C for 20 minutes.

4.  Remove the paper and replace with the tomato tops. Return to the oven and cook for a further 25-35 minutes or until the filling is hot and the tomatoes are soft but firm.

# Roast Potatoes

This recipe can be cooked from cold but you may need to add about 5-10 minutes to the cooking time.

*Serves 4*

*Preparation and Cooking Time: 1½-2 hours*

**4 large potatoes with a total weight of 900g/2 lb, peeled and cut in half lengthways**
**8 tbsp vegetable oil**
**Salt**

1.  Place the potatoes in a pan with sufficient salted water to cover. Cover and cook for 15 minutes until the potatoes are partially cooked.

2.  Drain the potatoes and place in a roasting tin measuring 17.5 × 20.5cm/7 × 9 inches. Pour the oil into the tin and turn the potatoes in the oil. Sprinkle with salt.

3.  Roast in a preheated oven at 170°C for 1-1½ hours, depending on the size of the potatoes, or until cooked, crisp and brown.

# Jacket Potatoes

This recipe can be cooked from cold but you may need to add about 5-10 minutes to the cooking time.
For a change, cook sweet potatoes in the same manner.

*Serves 4*

*Preparation and Cooking Time: 1½-1¾ hours*

**4 baking potatoes with a total weight of 900g/2 lb, scrubbed and pricked**
**Vegetable cooking oil**

1. Rub each potato in oil and place in the oven on a baking sheet.
2. Bake in a preheated oven at 170°C for 1¼-1½ hours or until the potatoes are cooked.

# Oven-Cooked Celery

This recipe can be cooked from cold but you may need to add about 5-10 minutes to the cooking time.
For more flavour, use a vegetable stock instead of water.

*Serves 4*

*Preparation and Cooking Time: 1-1¼ hours*

**Head of celery, with root and leafy parts removed, cut into 7.5cm/3 inch pieces**
**140ml/¼ pt water**

1. Place the celery with the water in a 17.5 × 20.5cm/ 7 × 9 inch roasting tin or casserole dish. Cover with a lid or foil.
2. Bake in a preheated oven at 170°C for 1-1¼ hours or until the celery is tender.

# Roast Parsnips

This recipe can be cooked from cold but you may need to add about 5-10 minutes to the cooking time.

If more convenient, the parsnips can be roasted around a joint.

*Serves 4*

*Preparation and Cooking Time: 1-1¼ hours*

**4 parsnips with a total weight of 550g/1¼ lb, roots
  removed, and peeled**
**Salt**
**5 tbsp vegetable oil**

1.  Cut the parsnips in half lengthways and place in a pan, cover with water, add salt, cover and boil for 10-15 minutes.

2.  Drain and place in a roasting tin measuring, 17.5 × 20.5cm/7 × 9 inches. Pour the oil into the tin, making sure you coat the parsnips well.

3.  Roast in a preheated oven at 170°C for ¾-1 hour or until browned and tender. Turn over half way through cooking if desired.

# Stuffed Aubergine

This recipe can be cooked from cold but you may need to add about 5-10 minutes to the cooking time.

Stuffed Aubergine makes a good supper dish but could be used as a starter or served as a separate vegetable with a main course. To serve a vegetarian, leave out the bacon, sprinkle with grated vegetarian cheese and brown under the grill after cooking.

*Serves 4*

*Preparation and Cooking Time: 1¾-2 hours*

**2 aubergines weighing 250g/9 oz each**
**Salt**
**4 tbsp vegetable oil**
**100g/4 oz butter**
**4 streaky bacon rashers, rinds removed, and chopped**
**1 medium onion, peeled and finely chopped**
**50g/2 oz mushrooms, chopped**
**2 tbsp tomato sauce**
**1 tsp soy sauce**
**50g/2 oz breadcrumbs**
**Pepper**

1.  Cut each aubergine in half lengthways and sprinkle with salt. Leave to stand for about 30 minutes. Rinse in cold water and pat dry.

2.  Scoop out the flesh and finely dice. Brush the inside of the shells with oil.

3.  In a pan, melt the butter and stir in the bacon, onion, mushrooms, sauces and aubergine. Cook for 3-4 minutes. Stir in the breadcrumbs and season to taste.

4.  Divide and spread the mixture between the cases. Place in a greased, shallow dish and cook in a pre-heated oven at 160°C for 1-1¼ hours or until the tops are crisp and brown and the shells are cooked.

# Stuffed Marrow

This recipe can be cooked from cold but you may need to add about 5-10 minutes to the cooking time.

Stuffed Marrow makes a good supper dish or a starter. Although the cooking time is long, the preparation is very simple.

*Serves 4*

*Preparation and Cooking Time: 1¾-2 hours*

**1 onion, peeled and finely chopped**
**2 tomatoes, skinned and chopped**
**65g/2½ oz fresh white or brown breadcrumbs**
**350g/12 oz minced beef**
**1 tbsp tomato sauce**
**1 level tsp dried mixed herbs**
**Salt and pepper**
**900g/2 lb marrow, washed, cut into four rings and seeds**
**  removed**

1.  Mix together the onion, tomatoes, breadcrumbs, beef, tomato sauce, herbs and salt and pepper to taste. Spoon the mixture into the marrow rings.

2.  Place in a greased baking tin measuring, 17.5 × 22.5cm/7 × 9 inches. Cover and bake in a preheated oven at 160°C for 1½-1¾ hours. Remove the cover for the last 15 minutes of cooking. Avoid overcooking as the marrow contains a lot of water and may collapse.

3.  Serve if desired with a white or cheese sauce.

# Duchesse Sweet Potatoes

This recipe can be cooked from cold but you may need to add about 5-10 minutes to the cooking time.

Sweet potatoes make a change from the traditional Duchesse potatoes but, if preferred, substitute them with your usual ones.

*Serves 4-8*

*Preparation and Cooking Time: 1-1¼ hours*

**1kg/2¼ lb sweet potatoes, peeled and diced**
**25g/1 oz butter or margarine**
**1 medium egg**
**Salt and pepper**

1.  Place the potatoes in sufficient salted water to cover. Place on the lid and boil for about 15-20 minutes until cooked.

2.  Drain and mash the potatoes until smooth with the butter, egg and salt and pepper to taste.

3.  Using a large rosette pipe and piping bag, pipe 8 rosettes of potato onto a greased baking sheet.

4.  Bake in a preheated oven at 170°C for 20-25 minutes or until the tops are tinged brown.

# Casseroled Rice

This recipe can be cooked from cold but you may need to add about 5-10 minutes to the cooking time.

Although cooking rice in the conventional manner is quicker, there may be occasions when oven cooking is more convenient. To make a savoury rice, use meat, chicken or vegetable stock.

Always choose a covered bowl larger than the water quantity and use a ratio of 550ml/1 pt boiling liquid to 50g/2 oz rice.

*Serves 4*

*Preparation and Cooking Time: 1-1¼ hours*

**225g/8 oz long grain rice**
**2.4 litres/4 pt boiling water**
**¼ tsp salt**
**1 tsp vegetable oil**

1.  Place the rice, water, salt and oil in a 3.5 litre/6 pt ovenproof bowl. Cover with foil and cook in a preheated oven at 170°C for 50-60 minutes or until the rice is tender.

2.  Drain and serve as desired.

# Stuffed Peppers

This recipe can be cooked from cold but you may need to add about 5-10 minutes to the cooking time.

Serve as a supper dish for two or as a side vegetable for four. If cooking for a vegetarian, use a vegetable stock cube.

*Serves 2-4*

*Preparation and Cooking Time: 1-1¼ hours*

**2 green peppers, weighing about 175g/6 oz each, tops removed, cored and deseeded**

*Filling*
**1 small onion, peeled and finely chopped**
**15g/½ oz butter or margarine**
**1 clove garlic, crushed**
**1 tbsp tomato sauce**
**½ level tsp dried Italian seasoning herbs**
**50g/2 oz long grain rice**
**285ml/½ pt water**
**Beef stock cube, crumbled**
**1 medium egg**
**Salt and pepper**
**25g/1 oz Parmesan cheese, grated**

1.  Boil sufficient water to cover the peppers. Place the peppers and tops in the boiling water and cook for 2 minutes to blanch. Remove the peppers and tops and drain.

2.  In a pan, heat the onion, butter, garlic, tomato sauce, herbs, rice, water and stock cube. Cover and bring to the boil. Reduce the heat to simmer and cook the rice for about 15 minutes. If the liquid has not been absorbed by the rice, remove the lid and cook for a further 5 minutes, making sure that the rice does not scorch.

3.  Beat the egg into the rice and season to taste. Fill each pepper with the rice, sprinkle the cheese over and place in a shallow dish with 2 tablespoons of water. Place the tops by the peppers.

4.  Bake in a preheated oven at 160°C for 25-35 minutes.

# Roast Butternut Squash

This recipe can be cooked from cold but you may need to add about 5-10 minutes to the cooking time.

Squash can be cooked like potato. It has a firm texture and is slightly sweet. The skins are much tougher and I find that peeling them can be awkward. My solution is to cut them in half, remove any seeds and then cut again into pieces. Only then do I peel them.

*Serves 3-4*

*Preparation and Cooking Time: ¾-1 hour*

**2 butternut squash with a total weight of 1kg/2¼ lb, peeled, seeds removed and cut into approximately 4cm/2 inch pieces**
**5 tbsp vegetable oil**

1.  Place the squash in a roasting pan measuring, 7.5 × 20.5cm/7 × 9 inches.

2.  Spoon the oil over the squash, making sure that each piece has been covered.

3.  Bake in a preheated oven at 170°C for 35-45 minutes or until the squash is lightly browned and tender.

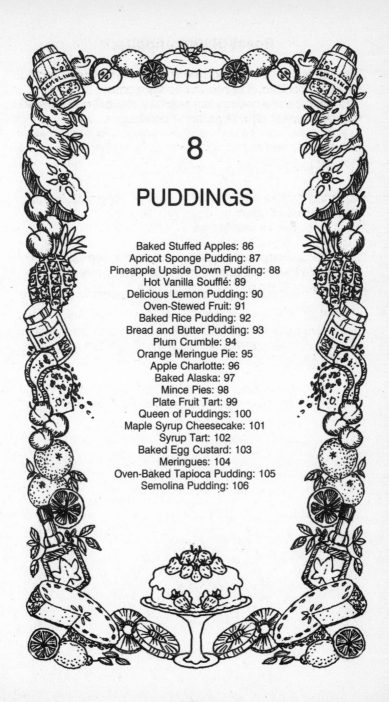

# 8

# PUDDINGS

# Baked Stuffed Apples

This recipe can be cooked from cold but you may need to add about another 5-10 minutes to the cooking time.

Instead of mincemeat, you could use 100g/4 oz of mixed dried fruit combined with sugar to taste.

*Serves 4*

*Preparation and Cooking Time: ¾-1 hour*

**4 cooking apples with a total weight of 900g/2 lb, cored**
**150g/6 oz mincemeat**
**25g/1 oz butter or margarine**

1.  With a sharp knife, score around the centre of each apple. Place the apples in a shallow ovenproof dish.

2.  Stuff each apple with mincemeat. Dot each with a piece of butter.

3.  Pour about 1cm/½ inch water into the dish and bake in a preheated oven at 170°C for 35-45 minutes or until the apples are cooked.

# Apricot Sponge Pudding

Any stewed fruit can be used as a base for this pudding.

*Serves 4*

*Preparation and Cooking Time: 40-50 minutes*

**450g/1 lb apricots, quartered and stoned**
**140ml/¼ pt water**
**50g/2 oz sugar to taste**

*Topping*
**50g/2 oz butter or margarine**
**50g/2 oz castor sugar**
**1 medium egg**
**100g/4 oz self raising flour**
**1 tbsp milk**

1.  Gently cook the apricots, water and sugar to taste in a pan for 15 minutes or until tender. Drain when cooked. Spoon into a 17.5cm/7 inch, 1.2 litre/2 pt buttered soufflé dish.

2.  In a bowl, cream together the butter and sugar until light and fluffy. Beat in the egg.

3.  Sieve the flour and fold into the butter mixture. Stir in the milk. Spread the mixture over the apricots.

4.  Bake in a preheated oven at 170°C for 25-35 minutes or until the sponge is brown and springs back to the touch.

# Pineapple Upside Down Pudding

For a change, use canned, drained apricots or peaches. Place them with the cut side up so that when turned out the smooth shape looks attractive.

*Serves 4*

*Preparation and Cooking Time: 35-45 minutes*

**225g/8 oz can pineapple rings, drained**
**5 glacé cherries cut in half**

*Topping*
**100g/4 oz butter or margarine**
**100g/4 oz castor sugar**
**2 medium eggs**
**100g/4 oz self raising flour**

1.   Butter a 17.5cm/7 inch sandwich tin and arrange the pineapple over the base. Fill the gaps with cherries, cut side up.

2.   In a bowl, cream the butter and sugar together until light and fluffy. Beat in the eggs one at a time.

3.   Sieve the flour and fold into the butter mixture. Spread the topping over the fruit. Bake in a preheated oven at 170°C for 25-35 minutes or until the cake is browned and when touched lightly with a finger the sponge springs back.

4.   Loosen the cake from the sides of the tin and turn onto a serving plate.

# Hot Vanilla Soufflé

There is no mystery to a soufflé, it is simply a flavoured white sauce into which whisked egg whites have been folded and cooked at once in a hot oven. As it is dependent on air rather than an artificial aid, the mixture relies on the gentle folding in of the egg whites.

For a variation, leave out the vanilla essence and replace with grated orange or lemon rind and a few drops of the appropriate essence.

*Serves 4-6*

*Preparation and Cooking Time: 50-60 minutes*

**50g/2 oz butter or margarine**
**50g/2 oz plain flour, sieved**
**285ml/½ pt milk**
**½ tsp vanilla essence**
**3 medium egg yolks**
**3 medium egg whites**

1.  Melt the butter in a pan, stir in the sieved flour and cook, stirring all the time for half a minute. Gradually stir in the milk, stirring all the time. Beat in the essence.

2.  Beat in the egg yolks until the mixture leaves the side of the pan. Set aside.

3.  In a bowl, whisk the egg whites until very stiff and, using a metal spoon, gently and gradually fold into the sauce.

4.  Spoon into a greased 17.5cm/7 inch, 1.2 litre/2 pt soufflé dish and cook in a preheated oven at 170°C for 40-50 minutes or until the mixture has risen to the top of the dish and is golden brown.

5.  If serving at the table, serve at once standing on a warm plate. If liked, serve a hot chocolate or jam sauce separately.

# Delicious Lemon Pudding

At the completion of cooking there will be a layer of 'lemon curd' in the base of the pudding.

*Serves 4*

*Preparation and Cooking Time: 1-1¼ hours*

**15g/½ oz butter**
**100g/4 oz castor sugar**
**40g/1½ oz plain flour**
**Juice and grated rind of 1 medium lemon**
**2 medium egg yolks**
**140ml/¼ pt milk**
**2 medium egg whites**

1.  In a bowl, beat the butter into the sugar. Sieve the flour and fold into the sugar mixture. Stir in the lemon juice and rind.

2.  Beat the yolks and milk into the mixture.

3.  In a separate bowl, whisk the egg whites until stiff and gently fold into the flour mixture.

4.  Pour onto a buttered 1.2 litre/2 pt soufflé dish and bake in a preheated oven at 160°C for 45-55 minutes or until a golden brown and firm to the touch.

# Oven-Stewed Fruit

Instead of plums, use the same quantity of prepared fruits, such as gooseberries, cherries, currants, apples or rhubarb, cut into 5-7.5cm/2-3 inch lengths. Hard fruits may need another 15-20 minutes of cooking time.

This recipe may be cooked from cold but you may need to add about another 5-10 minutes to the cooking time.

*Serves 4*

*Preparation and Cooking Time: 30-40 minutes*

**450g/1 lb plums, quartered and stoned**
**150ml/¼ pt water**
**75-100g/3-4 oz castor sugar to taste**

1. Place the plums, water and sugar to taste in a 1.2 litre/ 2 pt pie dish.

2. Cover the dish closely with foil. Cook in a preheated oven at 170°C for 25-35 minutes or until the fruit is tender.

# Baked Rice Pudding

This recipe can be cooked from cold but you may need to add about another 5-10 minutes to the cooking time.
  For a more liquid pudding, reduce the rice to 50g/2 oz.

*Serves 4*

*Preparation and Cooking Time: 1¾-2¼ hours*

**65g/2½ oz pudding rice**
**25g/1 oz butter**
**25g/1 oz castor sugar**
**Few drops vanilla essence**
**550ml/1 pt milk**
**Grated nutmeg**

1.   Stir together the rice, butter, sugar, essence and milk. Pour into a 1.2 litre/2 pt pie dish.

2.   Cover closely with foil and bake in a preheated oven at 140°C for 1¼ hours.

3.   Remove the foil, stir and sprinkle with nutmeg. Return to the oven and cook uncovered for 15-25 minutes or until the rice has absorbed the milk.

# Bread and Butter Pudding

This recipe can be cooked from cold but you may need to add about another 5-10 minutes to the cooking time.

It is a useful way to use up stale bread. If preferred, use brown sugar instead of castor sugar.

*Serves 4*

*Preparation and Cooking Time: 45-55 minutes*

**6 slices of white bread, 5mm/¼ in thick**
**50g/2 oz butter or margarine**
**2 medium eggs**
**50g/2 oz castor sugar**
**Few drops vanilla essence**
**285ml/½ pt milk**
**150g/6 oz mixed dried fruit**

1. Remove the crusts from the bread and discard. Cut the bread in half diagonally. Butter each slice.

2. In a bowl, beat together the eggs, sugar, essence and milk.

3. In a buttered 1.2 litre/2 pt pie dish, layer the bread and fruit, finishing with a layer of bread.

4. Pour over the milk mixture and bake in a preheated oven at 170°C for 30-40 minutes or until puffy, browned and all the milk has been absorbed.

# Plum Crumble

This recipe can be cooked from cold but you may need to add about another 5-10 minutes to the cooking time.

Apples can be substituted for the plums to make an apple crumble.

*Serves 4*

*Preparation and Cooking Time: 1½-2 hours*

**675g/1½ lb plums, quartered and stoned**
**100-125g/4-5 oz castor sugar to taste**

*Topping*
**100g/4 oz plain flour**
**Pinch salt**
**50g/2 oz butter or margarine**
**100g/4 oz brown or castor sugar**
**25g/1 oz desiccated coconut, optional**

1. Place the plums in a buttered 1.2 litre/2 pt pie dish. Sprinkle over sugar to taste.

2. In a bowl, sieve together the flour and salt. Rub in the butter and sugar until the mixture looks like fine bread-crumbs. Stir in the coconut.

3. Spread the mixture over the fruit. Stand the dish on a baking sheet to retain any spillage should the fruit boil over. Bake in a preheated oven at 160°C for 1-1¼ hours or until the fruit is cooked and the top is crisp.

# Orange Meringue Pie

This makes a change from lemon pie. Use either freshly squeezed oranges or shop-bought juice. To save time, a shop-bought precooked flan case could be used.

*Serves 4*

*Preparation and Cooking Time: 40-55 minutes*

**225g/8 oz frozen shortcrust pastry, thawed**

*Filling*
**300ml/½ pt orange juice**
**Grated rind of an orange, optional**
**2 level tbsp cornflour**
**50g/2 oz butter**
**2 medium egg yolks**
**100g/4 oz castor sugar**

*Topping*
**2 medium egg whites**
**100g/4 oz castor sugar**

1.  On a floured board, roll out the pastry to fit a 17.5cm/ 7 inch flan case. Bake blind in a preheated oven at 170°C for 12-18 minutes or until cooked.

2.  Meanwhile, in a pan, bring half the juice with the rind to the boil. In a bowl, mix the remaining juice with the cornflour to make a smooth paste. Pour the boiling juice into the cornflour mixture and return to the heat to bring to the boil, stirring all the time.

3.  Remove from the heat and beat in the butter, yolks and sugar. Pour into the flan case.

4.  In a separate bowl, whisk the whites until stiff and fold in the sugar. Spread the meringue over the orange mixture. Bake at 150°C for 12-18 minutes or until the meringue is brown.

# Apple Charlotte

Either stale or fresh bread can be used. Although this dish contains simple ingredients, it is a delicious pudding with crispy buttered bread and a soft sweet filling.

*Serves 4*

*Preparation and Cooking Time: 50-60 minutes*

**450g/1 lb apples, peeled, cored and thinly sliced**
**75g/3 oz castor sugar to taste**
**75g/3 oz butter or margarine**
**140ml/¼ pt water**
**Juice and grated rind of a lemon**
**3 medium egg yolks**
**5 slices bread, 5mm/¼ inch thick**

1.   In a pan, gently stew the apples, sugar to taste, 25g/ 1 oz butter in the water until cooked. Mash well and beat in the juice, lemon rind and egg yolks.

2.   Remove the crusts from the bread and cut each slice into three fingers.

3.   In a separate pan, melt the remaining butter. Dip each finger of bread into the butter. Set aside five fingers and with the remaining bread line a 1.2 litre/2 pt buttered soufflé dish.

4.   Pour the apple mixture into the centre and cover with the five bread fingers. Bake in a preheated oven at 170°C for 25-35 minutes or until the bread is crisp and brown.

# Baked Alaska

The secret of success in keeping the ice cream solid is to use the meringue as an insulator from the heat, just make sure that the ice cream is totally covered by the meringue, leave the completion of the pudding until the last moment and have the oven ready.

*Serves 4*

*Preparation and Cooking Time: 20-35 minutes*

*Base*
**15cm/6 inch sponge flan case**
**225g/8 oz can of fruit**
**2 tbsp strawberry jam**

*Meringue*
**¼ tsp cream of tartar**
**3 medium egg whites**
**3 level tsp castor sugar**

**Block of hard vanilla ice cream measuring**
   **8.5 × 8.5cm/3½ × 3½ inches**

**Castor sugar for dredging**

1. Place the flan on a shallow ovenproof plate. Sprinkle over a little fruit juice from the can and spread with the jam. Spoon over the drained canned fruit.

2. In a bowl, whisk the cream of tartar with the egg whites until very stiff. Fold in the sugar.

3. Place the ice cream on the fruit and smother the whole with the meringue. Make sure that the ice cream is completely covered. Dredge with castor sugar.

4. Bake in a preheated oven at 190°C for 3-5 minutes or until the meringue is a golden brown.

# Mince Pies

These are traditionally served warm at Christmas with custard, cream, rum or brandy butter. To 'pep up' the mincemeat, stir in one or two teaspoons of rum or brandy before using.

*Makes 12*

*Preparation and Cooking Time: 30-40 minutes*

**225g/8 oz frozen shortcrust pastry, thawed**
**75g/3 oz mincemeat**

*Glaze*
**1 medium egg, beaten**
**Castor sugar for dredging**

1.  On a floured board, thinly roll out the pastry. Using a 6cm/2½ inch pastry cutter, cut 24 rounds.

2.  Using a 12 portion patty or bun tin, line each of the bases with the pastry. Place a small teaspoon of mincemeat into each case.

3.  Dampen the edges of the pastry cases and place on the remaining pastry rounds. Press down the edges to seal.

4.  Brush each pastry with egg and sprinkle with sugar. Make a slit in each to allow the steam to escape. Bake in a preheated oven at 190°C for 12-18 minutes or until the pastry is golden brown.

5.  Remove from the oven and serve, or place the pies on a wire cooling tray to cool.

# Plate Fruit Tart

For a variation, use prepared gooseberries, plums or fresh apricots, and leave out the cloves.

*Serves 4-6*

*Preparation and Cooking Time: 40-50 minutes*

**350g/12 oz frozen shortcrust pastry, thawed**
**450g/1 lb apples, peeled, cored and thinly sliced**
**75g/3 oz castor sugar to taste**
**6 cloves, optional**

*Glaze*
**1 medium egg, beaten**
**Castor sugar**

1.  Divide the pastry into two and, on a floured board, thinly roll out each to fit a round ovenproof plate with a 22.5cm/9 inch diameter.

2.  Cover the plate with one piece of pastry. Brush the edge with egg and arrange the apples in the centre. Sprinkle over the sugar to taste and scatter over the cloves.

3.  Place the second piece of pastry over the apples and press the edges to seal. Trim the edges and press lightly with a fork to make a pattern.

4.  Brush with egg, dredge with sugar, make a slit in the top and bake in a preheated oven at 190°C for 25-35 minutes or until brown.

# Queen of Puddings

When cooked, the base mixture is light and has a taste of egg custard.

*Serves 4-5*

*Preparation and Cooking Time: 1¼-1½ hours*

**550ml/1 pt milk**
**2 level tsp castor sugar**
**½ tsp lemon essence**
**75g/3 oz fresh white breadcrumbs**
**2 medium egg yolks**
**2-3 tbsp jam**

*Topping*
**2 medium egg whites**
**50g/2 oz castor sugar**
**Castor sugar for dredging**

1.  In a pan, warm the milk and stir in the sugar and essence. Place the breadcrumbs in a bowl and pour over the milk. Leave to stand for 30 minutes.

2.  Stir in the egg yolks and pour the mixture into a buttered 1.2 litre/2 pt pie dish. Bake in a preheated oven at 160°C for 35-40 minutes or until the mixture is set and the top has formed a skin. Remove from the oven.

3.  Warm the jam in a pan. In a separate bowl, whisk the egg whites until stiff and fold in the sugar.

4.  Drizzle the jam over the pudding and then gently spread the meringue over the top. Sprinkle with sugar and return to the oven for 6-8 minutes or until the meringue is browned.

# Maple Syrup Cheesecake

This recipe can be cooked from cold but you may need to add about 5-10 minutes to the cooking time.

If preferred, substitute the walnuts with other nuts of your choice or with sultanas.

The biscuit base is crumbly so serve from the flan case. If preferred, use 225g/8 oz shortcrust pastry.

*Serves 6-8*

*Preparation and Cooking Time: 1-1¼ hours*

*Base*
**50g/2 oz butter or margarine**
**225g/8 oz digestive biscuits, crushed**

*Filling*
**450g/1 lb cream cheese**
**2 medium eggs**
**2 tbsp maple syrup**
**25g/1 oz walnuts, chopped**

1.  In a pan, melt the butter and stir in the biscuits. Using the back of a large spoon, line the sides and base of a 21.5cm/8½ inch flan case. Place in a refrigerator for about 30 minutes.

2.  In a bowl, cream the cheese, beat in the eggs and stir in the syrup and walnuts.

3.  Spoon into the flan case, smooth over and bake in a preheated oven at 170°C for 20-30 minutes or until firm.

# Syrup Tart

For a change, substitute 15g/½ oz of breadcrumbs with desiccated coconut.

*Serves 4*

*Preparation and Cooking Time: 40-50 minutes*

**225g/8 oz frozen shortcrust pastry, thawed**

*Filling*
**40g/1½ oz fresh white breadcrumbs**
**230ml/8 fl oz syrup**
**Grated rind and juice of 1 lemon**

1.  On a floured board, roll out the pastry and line a 17.5cm/7 inch flan case. Trim the edges and, with the remaining pastry, roll out and cut thin strips to be used for the top.

2.  In a bowl, mix together the breadcrumbs, syrup, lemon rind and juice. Spoon into the flan case. Arrange the strips of pastry over the top to create a lattice effect.

3.  Bake in a preheated oven at 180°C for 20-30 minutes or until the pastry is cooked.

# Baked Egg Custard

With the addition of egg yolks there is less likelihood of curdling.

*Serves 4*

*Preparation and Cooking Time: 50-60 minutes*

**2 medium eggs**
**2 medium egg yolks**
**550ml/1 pt milk**
**40g/1½ oz castor sugar**

**Grated nutmeg, optional**

1.  In a bowl, beat together the eggs and yolks with 140ml/¼ pt of the milk.

2.  In a pan, warm the remaining milk and beat into the egg mixture. Stir in the sugar.

3.  Pour into a buttered 15cm/6 inch, 850ml-1.2 litre/ 1½-2 pt soufflé dish. Grate over some nutmeg.

4.  Bake in a preheated oven at 160°C for 30-40 minutes or until the eggs are set and a skin has formed on the top of the custard.

# Meringues

To ensure that the egg whites will whisk, no trace of yolk should be in the whites, and the bowl and the beaters must be free of grease or water. Long very slow cooking is needed to keep the meringue white and dry so the lowest oven setting is the best to use.

I check if the meringues are dry inside by turning one upside down and gently piercing with a knife; if it comes out sticky, I continue to cook.

*Serves 3*

*Preparation and Cooking Time: 2½-2¾ hours*

**2 medium egg whites**
**100g/4 oz castor sugar**

*Filling*
**140ml/¼ pt double cream, whipped**

1.  In a bowl, whisk the whites until stiff and then whisk in half the sugar.

2.  Fold in the remaining sugar and, using a tablespoon, make six oval-shaped meringues on a non-stick baking sheet.

3.  Bake in a preheated oven at 70°C for 2¼-2½ hours or until dry.

4.  Cool and then sandwich together with cream.

# Oven-Baked Tapioca Pudding

This recipe is one which you either love or hate, depending on childhood memories. It is creamy and, as it is cooked in the oven, has a golden brown skin.

*Serves 4*

*Preparation and Cooking time: 2¼-2½ hours with soaking*

**100g/4 oz tapioca**
**690ml/1¼ pt milk**
**Pinch salt**
**15g/½ oz butter or margarine**
**1 level tbsp castor sugar**
**¼ tsp vanilla essence**

1.  Rinse the tapioca in cold water, place in a pan and pour over the milk. Soak for 1 hour.

2.  Warm the milk and tapioca and pour into a 1.2 litre/2 pt buttered pie dish. Stir in the salt, butter, sugar and essence. Cover.

3.  Bake in a preheated oven at 150°C for 1-1¼ hours or until brown on top and the milk has been absorbed.

# Semolina Pudding

Semolina is a germ or central part of hard wheats. Most of us enjoy it served as a pudding but in the early 1900s it was often served as a savoury dish.

A popular way to serve this pudding is with a spoonful of jam.

*Serves 2-3*

*Preparation and Cooking Time: 35-45 minutes*

**40g/1½ oz semolina**
**25g/1 oz castor sugar**
**550ml/1 pt milk**
**Few drops vanilla essence**

1.  Place the semolina and sugar in a pan and gradually add the milk. Bring to the boil, stirring all the time. Stir in the essence.

2.  Pour into a 1.2 litre/2 pt buttered pie dish and bake in a preheated oven at 170°C for 25-35 minutes or until a skin has formed and has lightly browned. Stir before serving.

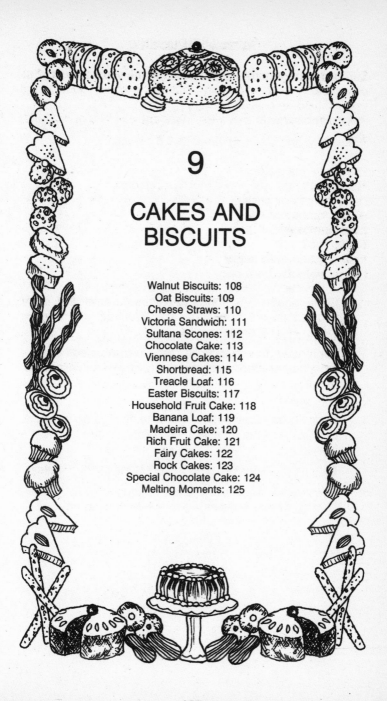

# 9

# CAKES AND BISCUITS

# Walnut Biscuits

Any nuts can be used – just substitute the walnuts with your favourites.

*Makes 20 biscuits*

*Preparation and Cooking Time: 20-25 minutes*

**225g/8 oz plain flour**
**Pinch salt**
**75g/3 oz castor sugar**
**100g/4 oz butter**
**1 medium egg**
**2 tbsp milk**
**1 tbsp granulated sugar**
**1 tbsp walnuts, chopped**

1.  Sieve together the flour and salt into a bowl. Stir in the sugar. Rub the butter into the flour until the mixture looks like fine breadcrumbs.

2.  Stir in the egg and sufficient milk to make a soft dough. On a floured board, roll out the pastry to a thickness of about 2.5mm/⅛ inch. Cut 20 biscuits with a 6cm/2½ inch cutter.

3.  Sprinkle the tops with sugar and then with the nuts. Lightly press the nuts into the pastry. Then prick with a fork.

4.  Bake in a preheated oven at 160°C for 15-20 minutes.

5.  Remove the biscuits and leave on the tray to allow them to crisp before transferring to a wire cooling tray.

# Oat Biscuits

Oats are back in fashion and these biscuits could become a household favourite.

*Makes 24 biscuits*

*Preparation and Cooking Time: 40-45 minutes*

**100g/4 oz plain flour, sieved**
**100g/4 oz rolled oats**
**75g/3 oz desiccated coconut**
**225g/8 oz castor sugar**
**6 glacé cherries, washed, dried and chopped**
**1 tbsp golden syrup .**
**100g/4 oz butter or margarine**
**1½ tsp bicarbonate of soda dissolved in 2 tbsp boiling water**

1.  In a bowl, mix together the sieved flour, oats, coconut, sugar and cherries.

2.  Place the syrup and butter in a pan. When melted, pour this with the bicarbonate of soda into the flour mixture.

3.  Mix well together and roll into 24 small balls using your hands. Place onto greased baking sheets. Allow a space between each to allow for spreading. Lightly flatten each ball.

4.  Bake in a preheated oven at 140°C for 10-15 minutes or until golden brown. Remove, and leave the biscuits on the tray for 5 minutes before transferring with a palette knife to a wire cooling tray.

# Cheese Straws

For cheese biscuits use a 6cm/2½ inch biscuit cutter and prick before cooking.

*Makes 32 straws*

*Preparation and Cooking Time: 25-30 minutes*

**75g/3 oz plain flour**
**¼ level tsp mustard powder**
**40g/1½ oz butter or margarine**
**50g/2 oz finely grated Cheddar cheese**
**Salt and pepper**
**½ yolk of 1 medium egg**

1.  Sift the flour and mustard together in a bowl. Rub the butter into the flour until it looks like fine breadcrumbs.

2.  Stir in the cheese and season to taste.

3.  Add the half of egg yolk and with one of your hands knead to form a smooth pastry.

4.  On a floured board, roll the pastry into an oblong measuring 10 × 36cm/4 × 15 inches. Cut into strips measuring 10cm × 2.5cm/4 × 1 inch.

5.  Using a palette knife, transfer the straws onto a greased baking sheet. Bake in a preheated oven at 170°C for 10-15 minutes or until the straws change colour.

6.  Remove and transfer to a wire cooling tray.

# Victoria Sandwich

If preferred, use a single 20cm/8 inch sandwich tin but you may need to increase the cooking time by about 5-10 minutes.

*Serves 6*

*Preparation and Cooking Time: 30 minutes*

**100g/4 oz butter or margarine**
**100g/4 oz castor sugar**
**2 medium eggs**
**100g/4 oz self raising flour, sieved**
**1 level tsp baking powder**
**Pinch salt**

*Filling and Topping*
**Jam**
**Castor sugar**

1.  In a bowl, cream the butter and sugar together until light and fluffy. Beat in the eggs one at a time.

2.  Fold in the sieved flour, baking powder and salt. Divide the mixture between two 16cm/6½ inch greased and floured sandwich tins.

3.  Bake in a preheated oven at 170°C for 20-25 minutes or until golden brown and, when lightly pressed with a finger, the sponge springs back.

4.  Allow to cool slightly before removing the cakes from the tins and cooling on a wire cooling tray.

5.  When cold, sandwich the cakes together with jam and dust with castor sugar.

# Sultana Scones

For plain scones, leave out the sugar and sultanas. For cheese scones, replace the sugar and sultanas with 100g/4 oz grated Cheddar cheese and 1 level tsp of dried mustard.

*Makes 8 scones*

*Preparation and Cooking Time: 15-20 minutes*

**225g/8 oz plain flour**
**Pinch salt**
**1 tsp bicarbonate of soda**
**2 tsp cream of tartar**
**2 tbsp castor sugar**
**50g/2 oz butter or margarine**
**75g/3 oz sultanas**
**1 medium egg**
**5-6 tbsp milk**
**Milk for glazing**

1. Sieve together the flour, salt, bicarbonate of soda, and cream of tartar into a bowl. Stir in the sugar and rub in the butter until the mixture looks like fine breadcrumbs.

2. Stir in the sultanas and add the egg and milk to form a soft dough.

3. Roll out to about 12mm/½ inch thick and, using a 6.cm/2½ inch cutter, cut into 8 rounds.

4. Place onto a greased baking sheet and brush with milk.

5. Bake in a preheated oven at 210°C for 7-10 minutes.

6. Remove and cool on a wire cooling rack.

# Chocolate Cake

Before cooking, this mixture will be very slack.

*Makes 8 slices*

*Preparation and Cooking Time: 40-45 minutes*

**25g/1 oz chocolate or cocoa powder**
**175g/7 oz self raising flour**
**Pinch salt**
**225g/8 oz castor sugar**
**100g/4 oz butter or margarine**
**2 medium eggs**
**100ml/3 fl oz milk**

*Filling and Topping*
**Jam or buttercream**
**Icing sugar**

1.  Sieve together the chocolate powder, flour and salt into a bowl. Stir in the sugar. Rub in the butter until the mixture looks like fine breadcrumbs.

2.  Beat the eggs and milk together in a separate bowl and stir these into the flour mixture.

3.  Divide the mixture between two 20cm/8 inch greased and floured sandwich tins. Spread out the mixture in each tin.

4.  Bake in a preheated oven at 170°C for 20-25 minutes or until, when lightly pressed with a finger, the sponge springs back.

5.  Remove and stand for 5 minutes before turning out to cool on a wire cooling tray.

6.  Sandwich together with jam or buttercream and dust with icing sugar.

# Viennese Cakes

To hold the shapes of the paper cases, place them in an individual bun or cake tray rather than on a baking sheet.

*Makes 12 cakes*

*Preparation and Cooking Time: 25-35 minutes*

**225g/8 oz butter**
**75g/3 oz icing sugar, sifted**
**225g/8 oz self raising flour**

*Decoration*
**Raspberry jam**
**Icing sugar**

1.  In a bowl, beat the butter and icing sugar together until light and fluffy. Sieve the flour and fold into the butter mixture.

2.  Using a piping bag and a large star nozzle, pipe swirls of the mixture into 12 paper cake cases.

3.  Refrigerate the cakes for 30 minutes. Bake in a pre-heated oven at 170°C for 12-17 minutes.

4.  Remove and place the cakes in their cases onto a wire cooling tray and leave until cold.

5.  Dust with icing sugar and place a little jam in the centre of each.

# Shortbread

If preferred, the shortbread may be cut into individual biscuits.

*Makes 8 pieces*

*Preparation and Cooking Time: 40-45 minutes*

**100g/4 oz butter or margarine**
**50g/2 oz castor sugar**
**150g/6 oz plain flour**

**Castor sugar for dredging**

1.  In a bowl, cream the butter and sugar together until light and fluffy.

2.  Sift in the flour and, using one of your hands, knead the ingredients until the mixture is smooth and comes away from the side of the bowl.

3.  On a floured board, roll the mixture out and shape into a 20cm/8 inch round.

4.  Place onto a greased baking sheet. Crimp the edges, prick well with a fork, and mark the top with a knife to make eight pieces.

5.  Bake in a preheated oven at 140°C for 30-35 minutes or until the biscuit changes to a very light brown.

6.  Leave the shortbread on the baking sheet for 5 minutes. Place onto a wire cooling tray. When cold, sprinkle with castor sugar.

# Treacle Loaf

To make a malt loaf, add 1 tablespoon of malt extract to the syrup and treacle. Serve sliced with butter.

*Makes 6-8 slices*

*Preparation and Cooking Time: 55-70 minutes*

**100g/4 oz wholemeal flour**
**100g/4 oz plain flour**
**2 tsp baking powder**
**50g/2 oz castor sugar**
**75g/3 oz sultanas**
**1 tbsp black treacle**
**1 tbsp golden syrup**
**25g/1 oz butter or margarine**
**140ml/¼ pt milk**

1.  Sieve together the flours and baking powder into a bowl. Stir in the sugar and sultanas.

2.  In a pan, gently melt the treacle and syrup together. Stir in the butter until melted.

3.  Beat the melted mixture and milk into the flour.

4.  Spoon into a greased and lined 450g/1 lb loaf tin, and smooth over the mixture. Bake in a preheated oven at 160°C for 45-55 minutes or until a small pointed knife, inserted into the centre of the cake, comes out clean.

5.  Remove and leave in the tin for 10 minutes before turning out, removing the greaseproof paper and cooling on a wire cooling tray. When cold, wrap in foil.

# Easter Biscuits

If preferred, substitute the currants with sultanas but the biscuits will take on a 'knobbly' appearance.

*Makes 22 biscuits*

*Preparation and Cooking Time: 25-35 minutes*

**100g/4 oz butter**
**75g/3 oz castor sugar**
**½ egg, lightly beaten**
**150g/6 oz plain flour**
**Pinch salt**
**¼ tsp cinnamon**
**50g/2 oz currants**

1.  In a bowl, cream the butter and sugar together until light and fluffy. Beat in the half egg.

2.  Sieve together the flour, salt and cinnamon. Mix into the butter mixture and, using one of your hands, lightly knead to form a smooth pastry.

3.  On a floured board, roll the pastry out until fairly thin. Cut out about 22 biscuits using a 6cm/2½ inch pastry cutter.

4.  Place the biscuits onto greased baking sheets, leaving a space between each to allow for any spreading. Prick with a fork.

5.  Bake in a preheated oven at 160°C for 10-15 minutes or until the biscuits have changed colour.

6.  Remove the biscuits with a palette knife and cool on a wire cooling tray.

# Household Fruit Cake

Not everyone likes peel so you could substitute the mixed fruit with 100g/4 oz currants and 100g/4 oz sultanas.

*Makes 8 pieces*

*Preparation and Cooking Time: 2-2½ hours*

**150g/6 oz butter or margarine**
**150g/6 oz castor sugar**
**3 medium eggs**
**100g/4 oz plain flour**
**100g/4 oz self raising flour**
**Pinch salt**
**½ tsp mixed spices**
**225g/8 oz mixed fruit**

1. In a bowl, cream the butter and sugar together until light and fluffy. Beat in the eggs one at a time.

2. Sieve together the flours, salt and spices, and fold into the butter mixture. Stir in the fruit.

3. Spoon into a greased and lined 17.5cm/7 inch deep cake tin. Bake in a preheated oven at 130°C for 1½-1¾ hours. Remove and leave in the tin for 5 minutes before turning onto a wire cooling tray. Remove the grease-proof paper and leave to stand until cold.

# Banana Loaf

To make a banana and nut loaf, add 2 level tablespoons of chopped nuts after beating in the banana.

*Makes 8 slices*

*Preparation and Cooking Time: 2-2½ hours*

**100g/4 oz butter or margarine**
**150g/6 oz castor sugar**
**2 medium eggs**
**450g/1 lb bananas, peeled and mashed**
**Few drops of banana essence, optional**
**225g/8 oz self raising flour**

1.  In a bowl, cream the butter and sugar until light and fluffy. Beat in the eggs one at a time.

2.  Beat in the banana with the essence.

3.  Sieve the flour and fold into the banana mixture.

4.  Line a greased 900g/2 lb loaf tin with greaseproof paper. Spoon in the mixture and smooth it.

5.  Bake in a preheated oven at 150°C for 1-1¼ hours or until golden brown and when a small pointed knife inserted into the centre of the cake comes out clean.

6.  Remove and leave in the tin for 5 minutes. Loosen the sides and turn out onto a wire cooling tray. Remove the greaseproof paper and leave to stand until cold.

# Madeira Cake

When cooked, the cake should be slightly domed with slight cracks on the top.

To make a coconut cake: Leave out the lemon peel and rind and stir in 50g/2 oz of desiccated coconut with 2 tablespoons of milk after adding the flour and salt.

*Makes 8 slices*

*Preparation and Cooking Time: 1 hour*

**150g/6 oz butter or margarine**
**150g/6 oz castor sugar**
**3 medium eggs**
**100g/4 oz self raising flour, sieved**
**100g/4 oz plain flour, sieved**
**Pinch of salt**
**Grated rind of 1 lemon**
**2 strips of lemon peel**

1.  In a bowl, cream the butter and sugar together until light and fluffy. Beat in the eggs one at a time.

2.  Fold in the sieved flours, salt and lemon rind.

3.  Place the mixture in a greased and lined 18cm/7 inch deep cake tin, lightly level the mixture and place the strips of lemon peel in the centre. Bake in a preheated oven at 130°C for 1½-1¾ hours or until when a small pointed knife, inserted into the centre of the cake, comes out clean.

4.  Leave the cake to cool for 3-4 minutes before turning it out onto a wire cooling tray and removing the grease-proof paper.

# Rich Fruit Cake

This is a cake for fruit cake lovers and can be decorated for a birthday cake. It keeps well for weeks in an airtight container. I have French friends who love it so much that they will not share a slice with any of their friends.

*Makes 12 slices*

*Preparation and Cooking Time: 3-3½ hours*

**250g/9 oz butter or margarine**
**250g/9 oz soft brown sugar**
**4 medium eggs**
**1 tbsp milk**
**Few drops vanilla essence**
**350g/12 oz plain flour**
**Pinch salt**
**¾ tsp mixed spice**
**½ tsp grated lemon rind**
**900g/2 lb mixed dried fruit**
**100g/4 oz glacé cherries, chopped**
**100g/4 oz mixed nuts, chopped**
**1 level tbsp desiccated coconut**

1.  In a bowl, cream the butter and sugar together until light and fluffy.

2.  Beat in the eggs one at a time. Stir in the milk and the vanilla essence.

3.  Sieve the flour, salt and spice. Gently fold into the mixture with the lemon rind.

4.  Stir in the fruit, cherries, nuts and desiccated coconut.

5.  Spoon into a greased and lined 20cm/8 inch deep cake tin and bake in a preheated oven at 130°C for 2¼-2½ hours, or until a small pointed knife, inserted into the centre of the cake, comes out clean.

6.  Leave the cake in the tin for 15 minutes before turning it out and removing the greaseproof paper. Stand on a wire cooling tray until cold.

# Fairy Cakes

To make fruit cakes, stir in 50g/2 oz mixed dried fruit after adding the eggs. For butterfly cakes: slice the tops off the cooked cakes and cut in half. Spread a generous quantity of butter cream over the cakes and then replace the lids at an angle to look like wings.

*Makes 24 cakes*

*Preparation and Cooking Time: 30-35 minutes*

**150g/6 oz butter or margarine**
**150g/6 oz castor sugar**
**3 medium eggs**
**Few drops vanilla essence**
**225g/8 oz self raising flour**

1.  In a bowl, cream the butter and sugar together until light and fluffy. Beat in the eggs one at a time with the essence.

2.  Sieve the flour and gently fold into the butter mixture.

3.  Using two spoons, divide the mixture between 24 paper cake cases. Place the cases in two individual bun or cake trays or stand on baking sheets.

4.  Bake in a preheated oven at 170°C for 12-17 minutes.

5.  Remove and place on wire cooling trays to cool.

# Rock Cakes

This is an economical traditional recipe and one which children love to prepare. Perhaps a good idea for a rainy afternoon.

*Makes 12 cakes*

*Preparation and Cooking Time: 40-45 minutes*

**75g/3 oz margarine or butter**
**350g/12 oz self raising flour**
**½ level tsp mixed spice**
**75g/3 oz castor sugar**
**100g/4 oz mixed fruit or sultanas**
**1 medium egg**
**Scant 140ml/¼ pt milk**

1.  In a bowl, rub the margarine into the flour until the mixture looks like fine breadcrumbs. Stir in the remaining dry ingredients.

2.  Stir in the egg and some of the milk to make a soft but not too sticky dough. Add a little more milk if required until the mixture is of the right consistency.

3.  Using two spoons, place 12 heaps onto greased baking sheets. Allow a space between each to allow for any spreading.

4.  Bake in a preheated oven at 190°C for 15-20 minutes.

5.  Remove from the oven and transfer onto a wire cooling rack.

# Special Chocolate Cake

This recipe was originated in 1830 by a Mrs Dunn and was passed to me by her great-niece. It tastes as good today.

*Serves 12*

*Preparation and Cooking Time: 1½ hours*

**225g/8 oz rich dark chocolate**
**225g/8 oz butter**
**150g/6 oz castor sugar**
**4 medium egg yolks**
**1 tbsp milk**
**Few drops vanilla essence**
**100g/4 oz plain flour**
**50g/2 oz ground rice**
**1 level tsp baking powder**
**4 medium egg whites**

1.  Put the chocolate in a bowl over hot water and heat until the chocolate melts.

2.  In a separate bowl, beat the butter and sugar together until light and fluffy. Beat in the yolks, milk, essence and melted chocolate.

3.  In another bowl, sieve together the flour, ground rice and baking powder. Gently stir these into the butter mixture until completely mixed.

4.  Whisk the egg whites until stiff in another bowl and gently fold into the chocolate mixture, two tablespoons at a time, until it is of an even colour.

5.  Spoon the mixture into a greased and lined 20cm/8 inch cake tin and bake in a preheated oven at 160°C for 55-60 minutes or until a small pointed knife, inserted into the centre of the cake, comes out clean.

6.  Leave the cake to cool slightly before turning it out onto a wire cooling rack and remove the greaseproof paper. When cold, serve either plain, dusted with icing sugar, or covered with glacé icing.

# Melting Moments

These are some of my really favourite biscuits. I used to cook them at school and they never reached my home!

*Makes 20 biscuits*

*Preparation and Cooking Time: 25-35 minutes*

**100g/4 oz butter**
**100g/4 oz castor sugar**
**1 medium egg**
**Few drops of vanilla essence**
**150g/6 oz self raising flour**
**Pinch salt**
**40g/1½ oz rolled oats**

1.  In a bowl, cream the butter and sugar together until light and fluffy. Beat in the egg and essence.

2.  In another bowl, sieve the flour with the salt and stir into the butter mixture.

3.  With wet hands, divide the mixture into 20 pieces and form each piece into a ball.

4.  Roll each ball in the oats and place onto greased baking trays, allowing room for the biscuits to spread. Bake in a preheated oven at 190°C for 15-20 minutes.

5.  Remove, and leave on the trays for 3-4 minutes before transferring them, using a palette knife, onto a wire cooling tray.

# Index